Henry Starr
Last of the Real Badmen

HENRY STARR
Last of the Real Badmen

by

GLENN SHIRLEY

DAVID McKAY COMPANY, INC.

NEW YORK

HENRY STARR: LAST OF THE REAL BADMEN

LIBRARY OF CONGRESS CATALOG CARD NUMBER: 65-19079

MANUFACTURED IN THE UNITED STATES OF AMERICA

To my agent
August Lenninger

Contents

Foreword

Frontier history is replete with stories of good-bad men and bad-good men. All were brave and fearless, and mixed with their wickedness were many noble qualities. Such a character was Henry Starr.

He was among the first of the old time saddle-and-horse bandits and the last of the real badmen. He practiced his trade off and on for nearly thirty years, and peace officers who had fought outlawry almost from the time the Five Civilized Tribes occupied what is now Oklahoma, declared that he committed more daring crimes in the days of telephones, automobiles, and many railroads than did the James-Younger, Dalton-Doolin gangs when communications were poor. His death-bed boast that he had robbed more banks than the James-Younger, Dalton-Doolin gangs combined was accepted as true by men who had known him since he was a stripling cowboy on the ranges of the Cherokee Nation. Of slight build, he had the physique of an athlete and moved with aboriginal grace. His most striking trait was his even, unexcitable poise, and the gangs he recruited were the most dare-devil in the Southwest.

Starr was born near Fort Gibson, Indian Territory, and buried within a hundred miles of his place of birth. But he made plenty of bloody history between the two places.

Yet, so far as is known, he killed only one man in his lifetime, and that was in a strange duel that baffled even the United States Supreme Court.

Only once was he caught in the act of robbery. This was toward the end of his career—after he had eclipsed anything the James-Younger, Dalton-Doolin gangs had done by robbing two banks in the same town, in the same hour.

Three times he faced what appeared to be certain death. Twice he was sentenced to the gallows; twice his life was saved by presidential commutation.

Three times he was to know the contentment of respectability, and was to produce a motion picture, *A Debtor to the Law*—his testament to the world that crime does not pay. But those who knew him best never believed he ever really reformed. He simply enjoyed raiding. He would laugh inwardly until he could hardly control himself at the enormous fright of his banker victims when he and his men would step in and take charge of all the loose currency with the "thumbs up and stand steady" that Starr always personally sang out. He was inclined to underestimate the danger of apprehension or death, and his reckless boldness probably accounted for his ignoble exit.

Nevertheless, he was a loyal friend and an intelligent man. He was educated in the Indian schools and spent the spare time between robberies with his nose in the classics, a supply of which he always carried in his saddlebags.

These features, without a doubt, stamp him the most unusual bandit ever to run loose in America.

Hundreds of books have been written on the James-Younger, Dalton-Doolin outlaws, but this is the first to be written on Henry Starr. There is one exception. While Henry was serving his second term in prison, he set down his own record of his early crimes in collaboration with a pioneer newspaperman, then threatened him with death if it was ever published. His story appeared, however, a short time later, in pamphlet form under the title *Thrilling Events, Life of Henry Starr; By Himself.* He details his many exploits "from boyhood to date." The most exciting part of his career came afterwards. He ends his book with a bitter tirade against society and with many comments on graft in the courts, especially in the court of the "Hanging Judge," Isaac Charles Parker. We'll see why later.

Although Starr's passions often were misdirected, his motives were honest—which is clearly indicated in his own story—showing a deep-rooted contempt for the white aggressor, and a cunning that was often his salvation.

I have tried to give a picture of conditions in the Indian Territory following the Civil War and the real reason so many outlaws, Henry Starr in particular, sprang from this section. Where appropriate, I have quoted from his own record as it was written more than a half-century ago.

GLENN SHIRLEY

Stillwater, Oklahoma

Henry Starr
Last of the Real Badmen

I

Leg Irons and Chains Make Their Mark

There are still men today who will tell you it was Henry Starr's misfortune to be born in the Indian Territory and grow up in the time of Isaac Charles Parker, the "Hanging Judge," when there was "no Sunday west of St. Louis —no God west of Fort Smith," and the most vicious gangs in the West roamed this wild country at will. It was called "Robbers' Roost" and the "Land of the Six-Shooter," and Henry's grandfather, the notorious old Cherokee warrior and outlaw, Tom Starr, did nothing to better its reputation. The history of old Tom's family is a story of blood.

Henry's father was George "Hop" Starr, half-breed Cherokee son of old Tom and brother of Sam Starr, husband of Belle, the outlaw queen. If there was an inherent criminal instinct in Henry's nature, it was a dark heritage from the Starr strain. His mother, Mary Scott, the half-

Irish daughter of Sterling Scott, a white man, was a highly respected woman.

It was popular belief then as now that a good mother will have a good son. But too often outside forces outweigh the influence of a good mother. This was true of the formative years of Henry Starr, in this land of Indian Nations civilized and saved from barbarism by the overflow from the States.

Henry was the youngest of four children. There were two girls, Adna and Elizabeth, and an older boy, Sterling, who died at birth. Henry came kicking and squalling into the world at daybreak, December 2, 1873, in a log hut four miles south of historic old Fort Gibson.

For years, Fort Gibson had been the farthest west outpost of the United States and one of the most important in the chain of military establishments reaching from the northern to the southern boundaries of the nation. At times, as many soldiers had been stationed there as in all the other posts across the frontier.

Originally established to curb the indomitable Osage, who claimed exclusive right to the game in all the surrounding country and waged savage warfare against hunters from the eastern Indian tribes, notably the Cherokees, the fort became, in 1832, the base of operations for the peace commission created by Congress to negotiate treaties with the wild Plains Indians for the purpose of locating in the Indian Territory the Five Civilized Tribes to be removed from the East. From its neatly whitewashed blockhouses and palisades on the bank of Grand River, Washington Irving set out with the Ranger company of Captain Jesse Bean on the first exploring trip westward, and from these experiences wrote his famous book, *A Tour of the Prairies, The Bee-Hunt,* and other stories. Captain

Nathan Boone, son of the famous Daniel, came to Fort Gibson in command of a company of Rangers under Lieutenant Colonel James Many, who led a second expedition as far west as Red River, the Washita, and the Blue. And with the Dragoon Expedition of 1834 came such personalities as Colonel Henry Dodge, Colonel Stephen Watts Kearny, and Jefferson Davis, then a lieutenant a few years out of West Point, accompanied by George Catlin, who painted many portraits of the Indians he saw and wrote a memorable account of the experiences of the regiment.

Sam Houston came here, in voluntary exile from his wife and the governorship of Tennessee, and spent three years among the Cherokees, sitting in their councils. He established a trading post on the bank of the Grand just across from the garrison, and became famous for his ability to consume much "fire-water" and the envy of every Indian and soldier in the region, before going to Texas. How Houston, with 800 men, inflicted a crushing defeat on a force of 1600 Mexicans under Santa Anna on the banks of the San Jacinto, and by this one decisive blow brought independence to Texas, is history.

No other fort in the West exerted a greater civilizing influence over so large an area, which included the Cherokee Nation. Surveys were made, roads built, and the migrating tribes settled in their new homes. There was good fishing in the rivers and thousands of prairie chickens and other game for hunting. The fort became the center of society and gaiety; plays were presented in the post theater, and the building was used for Indian councils and religious services on other occasions. There were horse races for high stakes in which all divisions of the fort's population participated.

The arrival of a steamboat up the Arkansas always

3

caused the greatest excitement. People flocked to the shelving of rock that made a natural dock to watch her come in with exhaust from her engines and the jangle of her bell. There was mail and news from the States and always passengers to come ashore—young officers from West Point, older officers on transfer to new assignments, recruits for the ranks, friends on leave returning with messages, and strangers to inspect. There were merchants with wares for which they had exchanged skins and furs in the East, sutlers with stores to sell officers and soldiers, and bonnets, dresses, and finery for the ladies. There were wives and children who came to unite long-separated families, and young ladies to visit relatives, frequently marrying officers they had met or had previously known.

The charm of the Cherokee maidens and their proximity to the post accounted for many marriages at the garrison. They were much sought after by the officers and were guests at all parties. Often, when their enlistments expired, soldiers remained in the Nation, married Indian girls, reared Indian families, and grew prosperous from the land holdings they obtained. Thus the quarter-blood Cherokee daughter of Sterling Scott met and married Henry Starr's father.

To Fort Gibson and the Cherokee Nation drifted also the criminal element. Many soldiers sought the excitement of the doggeries operated by mixed bloods on tribal lands just off the reservation. Drinking and gambling so demoralized the troops that the commanding officer forbade the soldiers to remain outside the garrison after retreat. Drunkenness and desertion became such persistent violations that the courts-martial inflicted punishment upon offenders as far as their imagination would permit, and, to enforce regulations, bars were employed on the windows

4

ín the outer walls of the barracks until they looked like dilapidated Arkansas jails. Such confinement at a post built to accommodate five companies of soldiers, together with the unhealthful climate where summer temperatures rose to 100 degrees, resulted in an appalling death rate among the troops and added to the ceaseless agitation to abandon the old fort and remove the garrison.

For years, the Cherokees had wanted full use of the boat landing, which afforded the only access to the interior of the Nation. They strengthened their argument with the fact that newer posts farther west on the advancing frontier had supplanted Fort Gibson in usefulness and strategic location.

The Civil War delayed matters. The fort fell to the Confederates. It was retaken by Union forces in April, 1863, and became the refuge of several thousand destitute Indians and Negro fugitives who remained there for protection and food rations. It remained garrisoned by four companies of the Sixth Infantry until September 30, 1871, when it was vacated by the command under General W. B. Hazen. In July, 1872, it was reoccupied by two companies of the Tenth Cavalry under Colonel Benjamin H. Grierson, who was sent to cope with the lawless element of the railroad crews engaged in building the Missouri, Kansas, and Texas Railroad from the southern Kansas border to Red River. The Tenth Cavalry stayed only briefly, and a company of the Sixth Cavalry and a detachment of the Fifth Infantry were assigned under Lieutenant Thomas M. Woodruff to aid civilian authorities in suppressing a gang of forty thieves and desperadoes that had organized to plunder and terrorize the country the year Henry Starr was born.

The only other protection afforded the Indian by the

government was the United States Court for the Western District of Arkansas at Fort Smith. The Intercourse Act of 1834 had attached the Indian Territory to the Federal Judicial District of Arkansas and clothed the latter with original, exclusive jurisdiction in all federal crimes except those committed by one Indian against the person or property of another. The discovery of gold in California, the advent of the Butterfield overland stage, the trade with the Five Civilized Tribes, and the coming of Texas cattlemen had brought so many whites to the border and so increased the court's business that Congress had divided the Federal Judicial District of Arkansas in two, the Western District including thirteen counties in western and northwestern Arkansas and all the wild area west to the Texas Panhandle and No Man's Land. Thus the Fort Smith court governed the largest area in the world, its authority absolute and final.

Towns and settlements sprang up along the railroad and to them flocked the inevitable refuse of humanity. The Indian courts took no cognizance of these "criminal intruders." Tribal laws had no application to the white man, and there were no laws by which a fugitive could be extradited after he had entered the Indian country. It became a mecca for outlaws of all races from the four corners of the United States and the most debased characters in the world. They committed bloody atrocities against lone travelers. Many banded together to defy the law and raided the cattle trails, settlements, railroads, and freight caravans. They made forays into the border states, robbed banks, stole horses, and pillaged. By the time President Ulysses S. Grant appointed Judge Isaac Charles Parker to the Fort Smith bench in 1875, the country had become a maelstrom of racial hatred, rape, robbery, and

6

murder that was to see the rise of such outlaws as Jim Reed, Belle Starr, the Daltons, the Rogers gang, the renegade Cooks and vicious Buck outlaws, and such unenviable lights as Ned Christie, Blue Duck, Jim French, Jack Spaniard, and Cherokee Bill.

In this atmosphere that reeked of tales and legends of the road Henry Starr was reared. "Looking back at it now," he told the Wichita (Kansas) *Eagle*, in 1921,[1] "it all came as a natural consequence—as natural as the moon following the sun. I was born as other men. I do not recall that there were any violent upheavals of earthly nature at the time, and of all those who remember the occurrence not one that I have plied but stoutly avers there was no unusual activity in the heavens. My early years were filled with such training and precept as a good mother will always give any only son. My sisters did their part, and right well it was done. Still, my surroundings, the very air I breathed, whispered of deeds of daring and peril and constantly called to me. I had the blood of Cherokee chiefs in my veins. Tom Starr, my ancestor, was one to conjure with in all tales of freebooting and lawlessness. In the '50s and '60s, he was known far and wide as the devil's own. In all matters where law and order was one side, Tom Starr was on the other, and his path of action lay along that scope of country where the Missouri line interfered with the Cherokee lands and stretched away south to the Red River. From my childhood, I was wont to hear the tales of his prowess and daring, how he was the one man with whom the government had made a treaty of peace, and my blood was fired and went chasing through my veins, burning and scorching me with the admiration of the thing. But even yet I do not think I had a desire to follow in his steps, though the freedom of the prairies and

7

mountains were constantly beckoning me to the free and independent life of the road.

"This much I tell you in the beginning, not as a matter of justification, for of that I make no search, but that you may better understand and weigh what followed. To you who live in the marts of the East or the more thickly settled sections, it is a language that tells you nothing. Your perspective is limited to your dooryard fence—to your fields at most; ours to the distance a horse might travel in a day with a rider up, whose nostrils take in the freedom of the plains and expand in the exultation of his manhood. To me, a child of the forest and stream, it was constantly singing me a song sweeter than everything else, appealing hard and strong to my wild, rebellious heart. There was constantly visions of the wildness, the living of it all, and it took hold of me, and always I was conscious of a never ceasing warfare against it. You are prescribed in your action by the laws of your king, while we—well, it had never come to us in that way yet.

"It was God overhead and nothing around. The world, our world, was ours and none to dispute. You must understand that our reservation at the time was inhabited by ourselves and there were few of our white-faced friends therein. Two railways [2] belted our broad prairies—these, and an occasional settlement, were the only forerunners of the teeming civilization you see today. We had been taught that it was ours, to have and to hold so long as grass grew and water ran, ours to hunt on, ours in which to follow in the footsteps of our fathers, to do with as we wished. That was the spirit that possessed us as a people. And certainly a small enough land it was, and is, of all the country inheritance had given us."

Starr explained it even better to a Fort Smith newspaper

while languishing in the federal jail in 1897: [3] "But a dozen short years ago, he with the blood of the Indian coursing through his veins looked toward the east, toward the west, the north and the south, and his bosom swelled with the thought that of all the millions of fertile acres, his people were the sole possessors. Then the Indian knew no laws but those of his own people and looked with supreme indifference upon the acts of the lawmakers of the United States. For the Indians had their own governors, their own wise lawmakers in their councils, their own judges and courts, and their own executioners, and the great United States drew neither respect from their honored braves nor terror from their evil-doers. They shot their own murderers and horse thieves and gave forty lashes at the whipping post to the hog stealer and the woman of easy virtue. Their religious ceremonies, peculiar unto this tribe for many generations, were carried forth with the same solemnities as before the face of the white man ever appeared to their vision—and the Indian people were happy.

"True, the white man was within their midst, but considered only as a vassal to till their fields and give a greater portion of the gleaning of the soil into the hands of the owners thereof.

"Then came the treaty with the great white council at Washington, giving forth in glowing terms the advantages to be derived by casting the burdens of their government onto the strong shoulders of the United States, and this looked good to the untutored men of the forest, so they signed the treaty.

"With the treaty signed and returned to the White Father, a great change came over the people of the Five Tribes. No more the mighty tones of their leaders re-

9

verberated through their council chambers, no more the alleged perpetrator of a crime was taken before a jury of his own people, who understood his temptations and his environments and tempered justice with the knowledge brought therewith. Instead he was taken to the tribunals of the despised white man, before a body of men who spoke not his language nor whose language could he comprehend, and here in a room peopled with strange faces he was told in a tongue whose understanding was beyond his ken that he should work the remainder of his days behind the steel bars of a prison cell.

"All this cast a gloom over the people of the Five Tribes, but still their faith in the white man's government did not falter. The treaty stipulated that all the lands of the Nations should be impartially distributed among the people of the tribe and a time was set for the consummation of the same. Likewise, the money held in trust for them by the white man's government and owed to them by this same government, was to be placed in their hands. But time dragged apace and the Indian had neither lands to rent to the white man nor money from the government, and their families suffered for the necessities of life. Gradually the government began to divide the lands and as fast as an Indian was placed in possession the eager white man took advantage of his distress and rented his hundreds of acres for a period of five years for merely enough money to supply the Indian's temporary wants. Then the United States government opened its heart and allowed the suffering red men $40 apiece out of the thousands due them from the treasury.

"And a great wave of despondency overspread the people of the Five Tribes. Naught was left to them of their old tribal relations but their religious ceremonies, and these were for a time carried on with frenzied fervor, but with the white man entering their country by the thousands and sneering at their misinterpreted ceremonies, even these were one by one dispensed with, and at the moment statehood is being thrust upon them, taking the last vestige of self-government from a once mighty people."

Of his early life, in *Thrilling Events*,[4] Starr said: "I spent my boyhood like thousands of other American boys. At the age of eight, I started to school, a distance of four miles, and I always made the trips to and from school on horseback. My teacher was a Scotchman from Canada—a highly educated and polished gentleman, but possessed of a most violent temper. All the pupils were Indians and four-fifths of them of mixed blood. In the early days there was no provision made for the education of white children in the Indian Territory. The tolerant Indian school directors allowed white children to attend free.

"I went to school to this bullet-headed Highlander for two and a half years, and am proud to say that I held my own with all comers in class-work. At the age of eleven I was in what I should judge to be the sixth grade; that ended my schooling. My father's ill health made it necessary for me to stay at home and I can honestly say that it was with regret that I gave up my books to help win our daily bread.[5] It was decided that I should try my hand at farming, so I hitched two horses to a ten-inch plow and literally dug into our farm. Critical neighbors said I couldn't plow; my sisters said I was too small to plow. This comment got under my skin and I made up my mind that I would not only prove to them that I could plow, but that I could also raise a crop. My furrows were neither straight nor regular, but barring whacks in my ribs and stomach from the plow-handles, I got my field plowed O. K., and

11

with only a few days help from a neighbor at critical periods, I really raised some splendid corn.

"This strenuous work taught me patience and self-reliance, and a stick-to-it-iveness that has been of great value to me all my life.

"In 1886 my father died, and a few months later my mother married a man named C. N. Walker, of Arkansas and Texas—a sallow, malarial, green-eyed reprobate who rented an adjoining farm. I had always looked upon the Indian as supreme and the white renters as trash who moved from year to year in covered wagons with many dogs and tow-headed kids peeping out from behind every wagon-bow, and who, at the very best, made only a starving crop. The Indian landowner was looked up to by his white renters, and always treated with courtesy and respect. But the years have brought about a change; the white man holds power, and the same hypocritical renter has grown arrogant and insulting; whenever the Indian is spoken to at all, it is with a sneer. The Indian, and especially the full-blood in Oklahoma, is an outcast in his own country, and it is with a feeling of sadness and apprehension that I think of his future. Broken treaties, misplaced confidence and insult have made him lose interest in life. I have more white blood than Indian, and with my knowledge of both races, I fervently wish that every drop in my veins was *red!*

"There may be a few good stepparents, I have seen a few, but I hold it does not pay to examine a snake's tail to see if it has rattlers. Walker was a greedy rascal who saw a fine chance of exploitation of rich lands, with free range and no taxes. From the first I seemed to be able to read him like a book, and we were secret, if not avowed enemies. He lost no opportunity to slip one over

12

on me by exaggerating to my mother my most trivial misdemeanors, and was forever complaining of my utter worthlessness and meanness. I confess I was sullen and inclined to 'talk back,' and if he asked me to do my work I complied with poor grace. Why should I work for this scheming renegade, when I *knew* he would take everything away from my mother, which he later did?

"He and I got along without an open rupture for about six months, but one morning he told my mother a deliberate lie about some trivial thing I should have done, and I very promptly said it was a lie. Such a thing was less majesty, in the opinion of my mother, and a look from C. N. was a sufficient cue. She ordered me from the table, saying she proposed to give me a licking that I should remember. I replied that I intended to finish my breakfast; then if she and C. N. wished to try to whip me, they could. I had always stood for her switchings as a matter of fact, but I did not intend that anyone should lick me over a lying stepfather. So when she came to begin operations I firmly pushed her aside. She called C. N. and the hired man to hold me, and by this time I was so angry that I told them I would certainly kill them if they laid hands on me. They could have easily over-powered me, but if they had, the stepfather question would have been settled for all time.

"Of course, this incident made things harder for me at home, and a few days later I ran away on the pretense of going hunting. I first went to a dance a few miles south, then to my father's sisters, where one of my sisters and her husband also lived. They were glad to give me a place to stay, and I went to work for them.

"About a month later my mother came after me, and I told her I didn't intend to go back; she was very angry at my refusal and tried to whip me. My sister and her husband told her that I was getting too big to be whipped, and as I was satisfied with my work, why not let me stay with them. They knew my home life had become unbearable since the advent of C. N., and shared my dislike for him. So mother took my horse and saddle and went home. It had always been the custom at home to allow the children to claim horses and cattle. I owned the pony and saddle, independent of anyone, having earned the money to buy them. A few weeks later my uncle by marriage came to see me and urged me to go back. Knowing that this uncle was my father's best friend, I listened to him.

"I still think his advice was bad, and can also see the fine Italian hand of my stepfather—the craven was afraid of criticism if I stayed away and begged my uncle to persuade me to come back. I returned with the understanding that no one would ever try to flog me. In January, 1888, we moved from the old home to the northern part of Indian Territory, about twenty miles south of Coffeyville, Kansas. Before leaving, my stepfather showed his petty, grasping nature by selling my pony and saddle.

"But the new country filled me with high hopes—miles and miles of prairie, where one could ride unhampered by high fences and timber. I aspired to own cattle and horses to graze on this fine range, and in the spring I began planting corn at 50 cents per day.

"My stepfather had two grown brothers (Jeff and Marshall) living nearby, and I must say that these two boys were as fine and honorable fellows as I ever met, and they both knew what sort of a fellow my stepfather was. Each of them had numerous chances to betray me in after years, when large rewards were offered for me, dead or alive, but they weren't that kind. And at this writing I hold the

friendliest feelings for the entire family, excepting C. N.
I cannot perceive how brothers could be so different.
Through Jeff, the oldest of the two boys, I got a job on
the Half-Circle Box ranch in the fall. My boss was James
S. Todd, an old Texas cowman, and one of the finest I
ever worked for. He was well educated and possessed of
plenty common sense, and I believe, even now, he will
testify that I was always on the job.

"Guess I would be working for him yet and all the
things of the past averted if it hadn't been for the following incident: One morning before breakfast, and just as
I returned from wrangling horses, I happened to be riding
the favorite mount of the man we were boarding with.
I met Todd as I rode into the yard, and he said that a
large number of cattle were about to cross the backwater
of a creek, and for me to hurry as fast as I could and throw
them back, as about a hundred had already swam over.
Now, I had always been anxious to serve Mr. Todd to the
best of my ability, so I forgot that I was on the favorite
horse of another man, and rode him at a clip to make the
sweat and lather come in profusion. About an hour later
his owner arrived, and when he saw his pet all but out,
he was wild with rage. I told him of the boss' order to
throw the cattle back without delay, and that I intended
to do it if it killed every horse on the ranch. We had some
words, and when I got back to the ranch I informed Mr.
Todd that I intended to quit, and why. He told me I could
work on if I wished; that the other fellow and his horse
were working for him and for wages, just the same as I.
But the bee was in my bonnet and I quit. You don't find
many as square as James S. Todd.

"I was idle only a few days. I got a job close by herding
some fine steers on the Open A. One day I went to Nowa-

15

ta, and a man I had known for four or five years was on his way to the Delaware Indian payment a few miles distant and asked me to take his grip over to the payment grounds. He had come over horseback and I was in a buggy, and pleased to be of any slight service to him, so I put the grip in and started.

"About two miles out two deputy marshals overtook me and commanded with drawn guns that I get down from the buggy and allow them to search it. I readily complied, and to my surprise and consternation, the grip contained two pints of whiskey. I told them that I had no knowledge of the grip's contents, also that I did not drink.

" 'So,' said one of them, 'then you must have intended to sell it, and that makes the charge against you more serious.'

"It was a penitentiary offense at that time to sell liquor in the Indian Territory. I did not inform on the owner of the grip, for I was satisfied that it would not help me. I knew that those scheming officers were stuck to make fees out of my bad luck. A United States court (the first white man's court in the Indian Territory) covering whiskey and misdemeanors had been established at Muskogee the year before [1889], and they took me there. That night, I, an innocent man, felt the murder-breeding leg-irons and chains.

"The men I was working for immediately signed my bond and took me back with them. They knew I was innocent, but advised me to plead guilty, pay a fine and have it over with, instead of fighting a long-drawn-out trial, with no witnesses to help me. When my case was called about two months later, I made a plea of 'guilty.' One of the deputy marshals, on being questioned by the judge, had manhood enough to say that he didn't think

I was a whiskey peddler. He didn't believe that I knew anything about the whiskey being in the grip. The judge fined me $100, a stiff penalty for the offense of introducing. I paid the amount and returned to Nowata, sad at heart.

"Though my friends all knew I was innocent, it did not remove the reflection from my character. I was lowered and cheapened in my own estimation. There was a tribal penitentiary at Tahlequah, the Cherokee capital. The convicts sent there by the council wore stripes, and as a child, the sight of them filled me with terror. My father and mother had brought me up to think it was an awful thing to be arrested. I felt doubly disgraced, being placed in jail and chained to a bed at the same time, and I was only a kid."

II

Henry Starr Begins to Ride

tarr went back to the Open A in debt, and "worked hard
and faithfully" until the fall of 1890, when he visited his
kinfolk at his old home near Fort Gibson, riding the distance of a hundred miles on horseback. Then he secured
work with a couple of brothers named Roberts, who owned
a small outfit in the same locality as the Open A. According to Starr,[1] "I had not been fired by the Open A people;
their cattle had all been shipped and there was nothing
to do. I rode for them again the following year [1891]."
By this time, he had become proficient as a cowboy and
developed an uncanny dexterity with a lasso, as well as
adding more skill to his horsemanship. He was five feet
nine inches tall, of strong, athletic build, with straight
black hair, friendly, intelligent black eyes, and handsome
with just a tinge of swarthiness. "I had blossomed into
manhood, weighed 144 pounds, didn't use tobacco, coffee

18

or liquor, and was very proud of that fact." [2] He presented every appearance of a youth who could be trusted.

"While working for the Roberts boys, two strange horses drifted into a pocket formed by two farms and a pasture joining them. As there was no water in this pocket, it was plain that they were runaways. The boys said for the first one who rode that way to let them into the gate to water, as no doubt someone would be on the hunt for them. I let them in and, not noticing that one of them bore saddle marks, I rode him several times. I also informed other ranchers that he was a stray. In something like a month, Charles Eaton, his owner, came after him, and seemed pleased to find him in such good condition, even offering to pay me for my trouble. This was in October '91, and in December, the same year, while I was in Nowata, a vicious-looking fellow, who said he was a Deputy United States Marshal, read a writ charging me with the larceny of Eaton's horse. . . . The warrant had been sworn out by Charles Eaton, the same fellow that had been so profuse in his thanks for the care I took of his horse, and that simply stunned me, nor do I know this day what made him prefer the charge, as he swore the truth later. I asked to send word to my friends, but was refused. I was taken to a hotel and handcuffed and placed in a room, the loathsome Eaton acting as guard. For supper they gave me a hunk of sausage and some crackers, and that night I was chained to the bed as though I were the foulest murderer. Even now, murder gets in my blood when I recall the cold chains on my innocent limbs. My faith in the majesty of the law and in my fellow man weakened, and during those long hours on my way to Fort Smith I was still handcuffed.[3] The marshal told me that a

19

certain attorney there might be able to get me out of this trouble, and as I was inexperienced, I took the bait. Hence, on my arrival I was conducted to the office of this legal vulture and gave him $22.00, all the money I had, and a bill of sale for my horse and saddle. Shame upon the fair name of our government for being a party to such a condition of affairs, instead of giving that protection pledged in sacred treaty to the Cherokee Indians; here was a commissioned officer of our government conspiring with a contemptible lawyer to cheat an innocent Indian boy out of a few hard-earned dollars. I shall not honor this lawyer by giving his name; he is only one of many of that stripe who disgraced that bloody and corrupt Federal Court at Fort Smith, Arkansas.

"From the attorney's to the jail I was not accused of being faint-hearted, but the sight of that old structure and the rough attitude of the officials chilled my heart. I could also hear the yells and curses of the 200 prisoners, who were allowed to scream as loud and as long as they desired. I was put on the second floor, the location for horse thieves and highwaymen, and no sooner was I thrust through the door than a bleached-out prisoner let out a series of yells and cries at me of 'Fresh fish!' whereupon the rest began to taunt me and laugh. I was hustled down to the 'Kangaroo Court' by this sheriff and a deputy, the sheriff all the time bawling, 'Oh, yes, the Honorable Kangaroo Court is now in session.' This business was all Greek to me. The 'judge' fined me fifty cents for breaking into jail without consent of the inmates. Of course, I didn't have a cent, and the sheriff knew it. The bleached-out, heavy one noticed a light gold ring on my finger, and made a grab at it, saying that the 'Court' would keep it for security. The ring had been loaned to me by my sweetheart, and to have that foul old jailbird even touch it was a desecration. I forgot that I was in jail, and smashed him on the nose and the sheriff on the chin, and we went at it for keeps. It was soon evident to his friends that he was overmatched, and they started to help him. At that minute a big, full-blooded Creek Indian came up and kept everybody off while I put the finishing touches to my man, and I certainly made him let out the big squeak. I was not tired nor hurt, and expressed my willingness to accommodate any of his friends, but they didn't seem at all anxious. Of course, this incident didn't make me at all popular with the sheriff.

"The odor of a large, poorly-kept jail is worse than the odor in the animal section of a circus, and this particular jail was the worst ever. I was assigned to a cell, the bed-clothes reeking with filth and covered with lice. I sat all night on a small box as far from the bed as I could get, and one never placed in a like position has no right to speculate on my thoughts. I, who had never possessed a cent dishonestly, and who had been taught to respect and revere the law from infancy—that a thief was a low, vicious person, and a jailbird one to be shunned—was put in among such men on a charge that I was perfectly innocent of, and was degraded and disgraced forever. In my twenty-three years since, I have passed through some pretty tough tests, but during the lonely vigils of that night my soul passed through its supreme baptism of fire. I am not ashamed to confess that I wept hot tears—not of fear, but of outraged young manhood. I felt that the future could never hold any good thing for me again.

"My cousin, Charlie Starr, a prominent cattleman, had heard of my arrest, and had me arraigned the next morning, going on my temporary bond. The lying deputy asked

21

the commissioner for time to get more witnesses. Of course, this request was a fake, pure and simple, but it was granted, and I was taken back to that vile cell. During the week that passed most of the good went out of me, and I became a soured, sullen man, brooding over this great wrong that was being done me. When no witnesses appeared, I was brought up for a preliminary hearing. Charlie Starr had seen the commissioner and explained my case. The scoundrel Eaton, who had sworn out the warrant, knew my cousin would not stand for a crooked swearing, and when he was put on the stand he swore to the truth, namely that he had offered me pay for taking up his horse and caring for him, and was forced to admit that there was a doubt in his mind that I had attempted to steal his property. Eaton was the only witness on his side, and I was promptly discharged. The commissioner gave Mr. Eaton and the deputy a severe reprimand in open court, but I can see now that this was only horseplay to appease the just wrath of my cousin. He should have had Eaton arrested for perjury and taken the deputy's commission away from him. I should have been given a hearing before being put in jail, and the reason I wasn't was because the deputy got $125 for committing me; he also got something like $40.00 for mileage, 50 cents for the sausage and 50 cents each for the breakfasts I was supposed to get, but didn't. Eaton received over $20 for mileage and $1.50 per day while waiting for the trial, making a total of another $95 or $100 that the government was out. A good investment for the making of outlaws. This ended my first introduction to Fort Smith's famous and infamous court." [4]

Recalling the experience, in *Crime Life*,[5] Starr added: "I crossed the [Arkansas] river as quickly as might be and entered my own country again, but my heart was bitter with disgrace and my brain surged and throbbed with thoughts and desires of revenge. And then it all came to me in a flash. There was the road for me; it stretched out before me, and I could see its turnings, its high and low places, and, in a dim sort of way, its ending, and I knew it was what I had been longing for and I took to it right gladly, feeling the spirit of exultation and freedom surge within me as my resolve was made. It was to answer the voice of the prairies and the mountains, and the blood of my ancestors was to have full play at last. . . .

"My resolve being taken, I lost no time, for in my chosen path, as in all others, delays are dangerous. The country was full of foal, fine food for the hungry jaw of justice I had left, merely waiting a leader to start as scurvy a band as ever put up a train or over-drew a bank, but reflection on the matter of taking the leadership over to myself gave me pause, and at last I threw the thought away, so that it came to pass I was accompanied by but two companions when I at last turned my first trick and faced the wilderness—a pariah of civilization. They were known as Ed Newcome and Jesse Jackson. . . ."

Newcome was a half-breed Delaware youth whom Starr knew in the country, "inclined to be tough and ready for any old thing." Jackson, a lanky, pock-faced man, sold whiskey around Nowata and always went armed with two six-shooters and a rifle. Starr claimed a "bare speaking acquaintance" with him.

". . . Whether or not it was the names their parents gave them I cannot tell, for roadmen have a way of dropping their names and taking others. With me it has ever been different, for I held the name my parents gave me to be as good as another and better than some, and I clung to it through good and bad as a thing not to put lightly aside. They had already won their spurs when I fell in with them and were playing at the great game of hide and seek with the officers. Railroads had a peculiar attraction for us, and it was but natural that we should fix on the [Missouri-Pacific] station safe at Nowata for our first venture. It was my own town, and I not only knew the lay of the land, but I also desired to prove that with care the old saying that a prophet is without honor in his own country might be set at naught. I told them how easy it would be to hold up the agent at night, as he kept open until 10 P.M. and was always there alone.

"Three days later we met by appointment. This was late in July, 1892. As soon as night fell we rode out from hiding and like a streak to Nowata—had less than an hour to make ten miles. We hitched in the stockyards and put on our masks, which we had made out of handkerchiefs. Not until that moment did we learn that a band of deputy marshals were in camp not further from the station house than a pistol ball might carry, but this gave us no pause and we took their presence as a joke. The night was of that inky blackness that all times suits the game. It was close on 10 o'clock and the night express had just thundered by, when we entered the depot.

"At first it looked as though the thing might take a serious turn, for in addition to the lone agent we had expected to deal with, there were a half dozen men in his office, though the waiting room was clear. In an instant fear that there had been treachery was gnawing at my heart. It is a fear that constantly faces all who play the game. I threw my gun into position for action and glanced keenly at my companions, and I read in their faces thoughts akin to my own. But the play was on, and though the odds against us had been raised, and for aught we knew the cards were stacked, there was nothing left us but to see it through. As it turned out, this incident which set our nerves on edge meant much to us. The little addition to the station force was the road's auditor and a party of his friends, and their presence added modestly to our haul. Fortune was playing on our side that night, but we did not know until later.

"The ticket window was open and two strides took us to it. Our guns were at their heads in a flash, and it was 'thumbs up and stand steady.'

"The rest was easy, and we lost no time doing the job well. Ten minutes later we were in the saddle, had set our 'barkers' to snarling and snapping so that our erstwhile hosts might keep their proper places until we should acquire a safe lead, and were riding hard and fast with spur and whip into the night—on through the camp of the court's minions, away to the westward—I to the Big Caney country, and Newcome and Jackson whither-so-ever the safety of the chase might lead them. For our night's work had given us a $1700 purse, and our thoughts for the while need turn only to the play of hide and seek with the sleuths.

"But on my wild ride this night, I met with an accident that came near being the end of me. The cattlemen in the country had begun to stretch their long tentacles of barbed wire, belting into pastures the great prairies for their herds. In my flight, I dashed into one of these where a few days before no sign of it lay, and myself and horse were dashed to the earth and cut and bruised most outrageously, and the wonder of it lay in the fact that we were not both killed, for we struck it in the darkness and fell head-on, and we were going like the wind."

In *Thrilling Events,*[6] Starr attributes this accident to a bad horse: "He bucked into and literally astride the fence. I slipped from the saddle and the horse escaped in the darkness. The other fellows had furnished the horse, but the saddle I had borrowed from a party in Nowata, and I knew I would be accused of the robbery. I came back to the location early in the morning and found that the horse had gone to a nearby house, and was cut beyond recovery. The farmer had taken the saddle to Nowata and turned it over to the authorities. Of course, the railroad detectives and deputy marshals soon had me under arrest, and off we went again to Fort Smith. This time I did not care, for I was guilty, but pleaded 'not guilty,' and my bond was fixed at $2,000."

Starr states, in *Crime Life:*[7] "Chief Harris of the Cherokee Nation, E. E. Starr, a relative, who was at that time treasurer of the tribe, and Ridge Paschal, attorney and politician, in whose veins also ran the blood of my people, stood as my sureties, and with but a few days loss I was back again on my own prairies, chuckling at the ease of my release, but determined to lay to heart the lesson my own carelessness had given me. I lifted [jumped] my bond, for 'twas no great task to find the amount most anytime, and it was safer withal than to let them get their hands on me again. So it came to pass that when November and the day of my trial rolled around,[8] I was in the country of the Osage tribe, 200 miles to the northwest, with one of the 'catchpoles' of the court who had thought it easier and safer to join me than to trap me, and I soon had two more tricks to my credit."

The "catchpole" and Starr's new companion was a man named Creekmore. "His parents had christened him Milo," according to Starr,[9] "and for months he was a deputy mar-

26

shal of the court, and, I believe, considered a good one. But his duties brought him into the reservations and soon the spirit that was over all had taken hold of him and he came to me as natural as a stream of water will settle to its level.

"This was September. I was staying at my old home near Fort Gibson, presumably to await trial. About November 5th, I decided to go to Nowata. Creekmore, who was staying at my aunt's, went with me. My lack of interest in my coming trial caused my friends and relatives to suspect that I intended to scoot to the brush, and they all begged me not to jump my bond. Of course, I said I wasn't going to, but I don't think I convinced them. We went to Nowata by train and had only a small sum of money. The weather was cool and crisp, and we had no horses or saddles.

"A certain old-timer, well known around Nowata, had said the first time I was arrested that all Indians were natural-born thieves, and I *might* be guilty of the charge. We were near his house this night, and to keep his opinion of the Indian from falling flat, I took two of his best horses and the only saddle he had. A few miles further I took another saddle. I had turned my back on established authority and resolved from that time to go the limit. We rode several miles and hid our trail and stayed all night at a friend's house. He told me that he had put $300 in a store at Lenapah, a small railroad town [to the north], and we decided that this was about our size, as we had only an old white-handled .45 and three cartridges between us. The next night we rode to Lenapah and took the farmer's hog money. It was a small enough affair, of a commonplace nature not at all to my liking, but it seemed a good enough trick on which to try Creekmore, and I must say that he acted very well, though, as it fell out later, he was in no sort fit for the life. We rode about sixty miles into the Osage country and got a friend to buy us each a .38-56 Winchester, new revolvers and plenty of ammunition. I also bought a new Cheyenne saddle from a cowboy. We turned the stolen horses loose and bought others.

"The day my case was called at Fort Smith, we were in a deep canyon far into the Osage, chuckling at the absurdity of anyone trying to arrest me. A few days later (at Sequoyah, Cherokee Nation) we robbed Carter's country store of $180 and turned again to the wilder country southward. A few miles from Wagoner, we stopped at the home of Frank Cheney. It was a cold, sleety night, and we were glad to get shelter. I had never seen Cheney before. Later, he came to be one of my men, and to make for himself a fair enough sort of reputation.

"The next day, near Fort Gibson, Creekmore bought a couple of quarts of whiskey and proceeded to get tanked. I objected and we had some words, and he got on his horse and rode away. The drink business didn't go with me; I had determined to always keep a clear head, so if shooting occurred I could give a good account of myself. I had already settled in my mind that I was not afraid of anybody." [10]

III

Henry Kills a
Deputy United States Marshal

When Starr failed to appear for his trial at Fort Smith, his bondsmen, smarting under the forfeiture of $2,000, offered a reward for his capture. At the same time, Stephen Wheeler, U. S. Commissioner for the western district of Arkansas, issued a warrant for his arrest. The warrant was delivered to Henry C. Dickey for execution. Dickey, the express company detective investigating the Nowata robbery, obtained a commission for Floyd Wilson as his posse, and the pair set out to hunt for the youthful bandit.[1]

"The railroad people put detectives in the field," Starr said,[2] "though what they hoped to accomplish I cannot tell, for you have my word for it, that it was no kind of work for a detective. Finding was easy, but there the work had just begun. One of the men, Floyd Wilson, went into the case with determination. He was, perhaps, a good sort in his way and brave he was beyond a doubt. Yet, he had so little judgment as to border on a fool. Of this point I shall presently leave you to judge for yourself. . . ."

Wilson was a tough, dogged manhunter, who had brought many a hardened criminal to the Fort Smith bar of justice. Contemporary accounts describe him as "a well-known officer, about 28 years of age, and at one time a rider with Bob Dalton." [3] Bob Dalton had the makings of a first-rate deputy marshal. He had done well while riding with his brother Frank. But he barely had served his apprenticeship before turning to robbing trains and banks, dying less than two months before at the hands of irate Coffeyville citizens.

Floyd Wilson, while riding for the court in the 1880s, often used Bob Dalton as his posse. Both were headstrong, possessed with fire and a desire for action. They made a good team. On one occasion, they had brought in Bud Maxfield and Carroll Collier, two of the worst members of the old Barnett gang. Barnett was finally killed by a posse under Deputy Marshal Dave Rusk, in January, 1889. Wilson was pretty much of a ruffian himself, but there is no evidence that he ever associated with any of the outlaw gangs. He was ill-tempered, quick to shoot for the most trifling excuse, and it was because of this attitude that he finally was dropped as a deputy. For instance, in January, 1884, when he and his posse, the Andrew brothers, arrested a man named Scott, Scott failed to recognize them immediately as officers, resisted, and Wilson lit into him with his pistol, beating him rather severely. After he was dropped as a deputy, Wilson married and seemed to settle down. For several months he had been on the Fort

Smith police force, and expected to go back to work for United States Marshal Jacob Yoes when employed by Detective Dickey to help hunt Henry Starr.

On their way into the Cherokee Nation, they met a man named John Keck, who warned: "The Starrs are brave, dangerous people. Taking Henry won't be easy. You'd better be careful."

Floyd Wilson laughed and replied, confidently: "The right man can handle him. We will bring him in alive— or dead!"

"They openly boasted of what they would do to me on sight," Starr claimed, in *Thrilling Events*.[4] "The night before the shooting, these fellows called at my sister's house to see if I was there, broke down her door and acted in a manner unbecoming to officers and gentlemen. The insults to my sister made me nearly crazy, and their threats to shoot me on sight brought about the killing. . . .

"I had ranged up into the California Creek country, the chase had eased on me and I became bolder, almost foolhardy in my carelessness, and it at last led to the dice falling once more against me. I had kept close in the bush since the [Lenapah and Sequoyah] affairs in November and it was now December. I say I had become careless, and no other word will do, for I had greatly relaxed my watchfulness and they had me to rights almost before I was aware that danger lurked."

On the night of December 8, Starr appeared in Coffeyville, bought wire nippers and gun holsters, and "escaped before police could catch him." Word went out that he had rejoined Newcome and Jackson, and the gang was planning to equal the record of the Daltons. Dickey and Wilson, who had been guarding express trains on the Missouri-

Pacific between Coffeyville and Wagoner, hurried north.[5]

On December 12, Dickey and Wilson picked up Starr's trail near Lenapah. They proceeded south by rail, and just at dusk arrived at Arthur Dodge's "XU" ranch, eight miles from Nowata, where it had been reported the gang was rendezvoused. Dodge denied that the gang was personally known by him, but admitted he had seen Starr ride past his place several times. On being apprized of the outlaw's presence, the officers mounted their horses and scoured the country, continuing the search until after midnight. The following day, as they sat at dinner with the ranchman's family, Dodge galloped in from attending affairs on the ranch and informed them he had just seen Starr ride past again. Wilson rushed to the stable, mounted the horse, already saddled and bridled, on which Dodge had just returned, and started in the direction the ranchman had sighted the outlaw. Dickey, forced to obtain a fresh mount, was delayed several minutes, and Wilson pressed on ahead of the detective to take the fugitive alone. He came upon Starr in an opening on Wolf Creek.

The two men sighted each other the same instant, and Starr dropped from his saddle, rifle ready. Wilson halted, and sat facing his quarry only thirty yards away, Winchester in his hands.

He ordered Starr to surrender, and the outlaw tried to "work away" from the officer.

"Hold up; I have a warrant for you!" ordered Wilson, and rode up to within 25 or 30 feet of Starr.

"You hold up!" called Starr, who made no further effort to flee.

Wilson then sprang from his horse, threw his rifle to

his shoulder, and fired over the outlaw's head to frighten him.

Starr had been standing with his gun in both hands, holding the muzzle down, but, upon Wilson's shooting, returned the fire, and continued to fire rapidly. Wilson fell, badly wounded. As he levered for a fresh cartridge, the empty shell jammed in his rifle. Throwing down the weapon, he reached for his revolver, and Starr fired two more shots. Wilson sank back on the ground. As he lay there, too weak to lift the six-shooter he had drawn, the outlaw calmly strode forward and fired another bullet into his heart, holding the gun so close that the blaze spouting from its muzzle scorched the officer's clothing.

The shooting frightened away their horses, but Starr managed to catch Wilson's. Detective Dickey, meanwhile, had failed to reach his companion. The fresh horse saddled for him by Dodge had objected to a strange rider and had "bucked badly, preventing the officer's arrival at the place of battle until too late." Starr mounted and leisurely rode away to safety. Dickey brought Wilson's body into Lenapah and from there took it by passenger train to Coffeyville.[6]

Starr mentions the killing only briefly in *Thrilling Events:*[7] "I killed him [Wilson]," and he erroneously claims that he "made his companion hug the ground so close that he played 'possum.' I had promised myself never to shoot unless it was to save my own life, and have never had any qualms of conscience over that occurrence. It was simply a case of their lives or mine. They started the fireworks, and besides . . . they were working for the reward offered by the railroad."

In *Crime Life,*[8] however, he admitted: "For the first

33

time there was blood on my hands, and I broke from my haunts, and, like a frightened coyote, drove straight into the Osage country, fear tugging at my heart and my brain afire. For a man is like a beast; fear drives him before it into the wildest spot, but also like a beast, in a week's time he forgets."

IV

The Starr Gang
Looks to the Railroad—

"Henry Starr, the young man who killed Floyd Wilson, is still at large," announced the Vinita *Indian Chieftain,* of December 22, "but his capture is expected." The most elaborate attempt to capture any single outlaw in the Indian Territory was made under the direction of United States Marshal Jacob Yoes, who devoted a full week to the organization and training of a band of twenty picked deputies. By Christmas, this valiant body of men, under the ominous title of the "Starr militia," was combing the Cherokee and Osage nations.

"Many were brave officers," Starr recalled,[1] "but their methods were ridiculous. They made several drives for me, much in the manner that cowboys made a drive for coyotes. But with a swift pony and thorough knowledge of the country, and all the noise and confusion they made,

35

I easily made their efforts useless. I generally followed the militia by something like half a day in the pursuit."

Starr had an even better point in his favor: "I scouted the country within a radius of 60 by 160 miles from the scene of the shooting and nine-tenths of the people were my friends. They knew I had jumped my bond, was a highwayman and had killed my man, but they also knew of my two previous arrests when innocent, and that I had to kill or get killed in the engagement with Wilson." [2] These people were honest, hard-working citizens, and although the majority were white men, who could easily have shot him while he slept, they chose to shield and stand guard over him.

"We have an axiom, us fellows of the fair and free, that a friend must needs be stuck close to," explained Starr.[3] "By a friend we mean those who would house us, provision us and, if need be, in the hours of peril, arm us, and always tell the sleuths who constantly hung on our scents, everything and anything but the truth." Many were actuated by sympathy, others by fear, but the result was the same.

Starr remained loyal and faithful to such men, for in their hands lay his safety. When danger was near, some friend was always on hand to put him wise.

"I wasn't playing the coyote, either," Starr wrote. "The two marshals who had arrested me when innocent, took to the tall and uncut, having found out that I was a dead shot and might remember, to their undoing, the large part they had played in making my life a wreck. . . ." [4]

"But I was scarcely going around with a chip on my shoulder. I have some pride. I never held the life of man cheaply. Even with the 'catchpoles' who dogged me from the first and at last came to hang on my flanks like beagles on a hare, I was ever considerate, and used my 'barkers' only when fate refused to show me other means to save my precious hide. I say it was precious, and indeed it was, in more ways than one, for it had come to be worth a goodly number of ducats to any man who might flaunt it, and many there were who sought to gain some spending money in this manner." [5]

He describes how he spared the lives of Deputy Marshals Ike Rogers and Rufus Cannon as follows: "I had met my mother and sister by appointment at the home of J. O. Morrison, on the prairie nine miles northwest of Nowata, and I heard afterwards my treacherous stepfather had told the deputies to get me. As they approached the house, I was undetermined what to do. At that time I was paying attention to Mr. Morrison's daughter, May, and in her presence I would not run. Perish forever the thought! There were several ladies present, and they pleaded with me not to kill the officers. 'Ladies,' I replied, 'it is not a question of my killing them but of keeping them from killing me!' I kept out of sight in the hall at the head of the stairs with my rifle drawn, and could have killed them as easy as shooting two rabbits had I so desired. Both knew I was in the house, for they had discovered my well-known horse tied in the barn, but at the time each assured the other that I was not any place around. As they started off, I watched them from the window. Rogers' hat blew off as he passed the window, and he looked up, but I had him covered and he only pulled his hat over his eyes and went on without looking back. They made no attempt at my arrest, and I could tell by their action that they did not want me very bad." [6]

It was a different story when Starr, with Ed Newcome and Jesse Jackson, his first pals, ran into Rogers and Cannon later that winter. The trio had split. While Starr and his new partner Creekmore were committing the Lenapah and Sequoyah robberies, Newcome, Jackson, and a notorious character named Ernest Lewis had held up the southbound passenger train on the Santa Fe at Wharton, in the Cherokee Outlet, and were being sought by deputy United States marshals of Oklahoma Territory at Guthrie. Starr often visited them at their hideout in the Osage hills. Lewis was a white man wanted for murder in the Chickasaw Nation and for killing another man in the state of Washington before fleeing to the Indian Territory. After quarreling with Lewis over their failure to find any money in the express car at Wharton, Newcome and Jackson decided to return with Starr to the Cherokee Nation. On the evening of January 20, 1893, near Bartlesville, they came upon Rogers and Cannon and a posse of "fifteen or more" Indian police, armed and waiting. A running fight ensued, in which Cannon "shot off Jackson's right arm and sent another bullet through his side before he was captured." Starr and Newcome escaped. Rogers, in his report of the fight to Marshal Yoes at Fort Smith, stated that "about two hundred shots were fired," the captured outlaw would "possibly recover," and "we are now on the trail of Starr and his confederate and will yet run them down. We are determined to rid society of this gang." [7]

Within a few weeks, Newcome was captured at his mother's home on California Creek, north of Nowata, by Deputy Marshals G. S. White and J. C. Wilkerson; Lewis was captured at Pawhuska, Osage Nation, by Deputy Marshal Heck Thomas of Guthrie; and Milo Creekmore voluntarily surrendered. [8]

"It was in the run of luck that both Newcome and Jackson should be taken," Starr said. "Their day was short after I parted with them. They were carted away to Fort Smith where in a short time they were turned over to the Oklahoma authorities and landed in the holdfast at Guthrie, where later Jackson took his own life. Newcome received the limit and served it like the man he was, and afterwards, so I have been told, answered the call of his country and went out with the forces to Manila to mix in with the little brown men, and here, for aught I know, he still may be today. But give him a chance and I'll wager he'll show the little heathen some tricks that will make their top-locks stand straight, for he had a way with him, had Newcome.

"Of Creekmore, I will say that he was brave and generous and possessed no little amount of intelligence. But he was foolish in combining two callings which were in direct conflict. He said he could not make any money riding marshal and besides he wanted to be a bandit, something on the order of Jesse James, but I had suspected that he meant to turn me in, and moved on without him."

Always on the go, always pursued, Starr continued to avoid the marshals. For the second time, he found himself alone, and hastened away to his old haunts on the Big Caney to the north, where within the week he received his next baptism of fire.

"I had known all day that on every side the officers were hunting me, and that I was hard pressed, but it was late in the afternoon before they came up with me, and even then they did not stay longer than was necessary. My road lay along the edge of the brush, and I was riding at a fair gait to make a safe stopping place for the night, when two men suddenly hove in sight, 200 paces in my front. At the first glance I knew that the play was up to me, and I reined in and called them to ride around. Their answer was to fall from their horses, which they used as breast-works, and open fire on me. But as quick as they were, I was quicker, and before their first shot rang out, I was behind my own horse, their bullets biting savagely at the twigs and trees about my head. I killed both of their horses and they took to cover with the alacrity born of wisdom, and I had but to change my course to throw them off the scent.

"I could have put them both out of the running, but what would have been the use? There were hundreds more to take up the chase where they would have left off, and the price of me would have been increased, and in that was danger. Then, too, there was always in my mind the thought that the time might come when I would be called to an accounting, and murder—well, 'tis a nasty charge to face." [10]

It was now that Henry planned the organization of a picked band "to show the natives just how real outlaws could perform." The newspapers had said so many bad things about him that he concluded "to make the editors truthful for once." This gang materialized later, as subsequent events will show, and was really the terror Starr planned it would be.

The first man he chose was Frank Cheney, the young farmer with whom he had taken refuge, living seven miles north of Wagoner. Just to "keep in shape" while recruiting other members of the band, they "rounded" the little town of Choteau on the Missouri, Kansas, and Texas railroad late in January.

They met with a couple of disappointments. They rode in to rob the 8 o'clock northbound passenger train, but arrived just as it was leaving the station. They held up the agent and four passengers who had just got off the train, obtaining $180, then rode over to Haden's store, where W. A. Hancock, a clerk, was on duty. The store did most of the banking for cattlemen in the area and usually had five to six thousand dollars in its safe. But Hancock had taken the money to the Vinita bank the day before. Starr cursed him, smashed out the front window with the butt of his Winchester, took $390 and left.[11]

A few days later, in February, they struck the town of Inola on the Missouri-Pacific (Iron Mountain line), "cleaning out the general store and depot and securing $220." [12] Ben F. Williams, the telegraph operator and one of their victims, remembered: "The bandits hitched their horses to the right-of-way fence some distance from the depot, then walked into Wood Hubbard's store, held him up and robbed him of his watch and money. R. E. Craig, railroad agent, went to the store to get the mail for a train soon to arrive, and they stood him up beside Hubbard and robbed him. The section foreman strolled into the store to get some tobacco and he was robbed, and then these three men were marched to the depot, where I was given the same treatment. Then they marched us out to their horses, which they mounted and rode away. My little daughter, Grace Williams, two years old, came into the office while Henry Starr was taking my watch, and stood by me. She was frightened by his black mask and whimpered. Starr told her not to cry and assured her that he would not hurt her." Years later, as a reporter on the McAlester *News-Capitol,* she included in a newspaper article about Starr the story of her childhood encounter.[13]

Frank Cheney returned to his home north of Wagoner, still posing as a farmer. Starr had determined never to allow anyone to see him at Cheney's place, and scouted north again, alone: "In February, I was going through the

41

Verdigris bottoms. . . . It was a winter night, though warm, and there was a dim moon in the west. It was about 2:30 in the morning when I passed through a thick settlement. Every dog in the country seemed to wake and bark. I knew that the barking of the dogs would reveal my course if anyone was out looking, and while I hardly expected to find officers after me (at that time of night) I proceeded with some care. I had friends in the settlement, but hadn't been in these parts for several weeks and knew they would not be expecting me. I came to a point where the road led north. There was a farm to the east and open prairie to the west, the high hills with timber showing down to the road. I dismounted and walked, my Winchester cocked and held in the direction of that timber. The faint moon was casting weird shadows, and while on the watch, my thoughts were on higher doings. If I had been an imaginative person, I could have seen all sorts of hobgoblins and bogy-men. The spell of the night and the solitude was over me, and I was feeling from the depths of my soul what the poets so weakly express.

"I knew there was a lane running east a short way ahead, and I approached it with extreme caution. I hope it will not be considered boasting on my part if I say that for keen sight and hearing I am there with the goods. I have failed to find one who could beat me in this respect.

"About 100 yards from the lane I led my horse under the shadow of some trees and went forward to reconnoiter. I sensed the approach of someone, and when within about thirty feet of the lane, I saw two mounted men coming from the east. I felt certain they had not seen me, so stepped up to within ten feet of the corner and covered them, at the same time telling them in language more forceful than polite that they had best drop their guns, ride straight ahead and not look back. They were scared to death, and as they rode away like statues into the night, I taunted them with the fact I was Henry Starr, bandit and dead-shot, and why not come back and get me and the $1,200 reward on my head. Had the situation been reversed, they would have sent me to the boneyard.

"I rode about a half mile to the east, and as I came to a creek bed without any timber, I noticed three men riding out of a gully not sixty yards away. I was off in a jiffy and fell on the ground; they, too, dismounted and stood behind their horses. I saw their Winchesters glisten in the moonlight, and why they didn't shoot, or why I didn't, can be answered by the savants. I suppose they, as well as I, dreaded the consequence at such close range. After a few minutes had passed with nothing happening, I knew I had the Indian sign on them. I told them I was Henry Starr and was ready to fight them to the death; that I had just disarmed their two friends at the head of the lane, and if they didn't back off, I proposed to blow them off the prairie. That there is magic in a name is proved by the fact that they mounted and rode on without having spoken one word. I immediately cut a wire fence and galloped through a wheat field to a friend's house nearby, where I stayed a few days." [14]

Starr's contempt for the marshals increased with his experience. The gossip among the country folk was of great benefit to him. Someone told that he wore a steel breastplate; another that Starr had shown him the breastplate and places where bullets had struck it. This talk, together with his phenomenal accuracy and swiftness with firearms, protected him from many a federal deputy and other official. Fred Sutton [15] claimed that a man told him he had seen Starr kill a running coyote with a rifle at 685 measured yards. According to Starr, this exhibition of his marksmanship occurred at the home of a friend, in the presence of several witnesses, and at the same time, he "shot a rabbit dead at 150 yards on the run." On another occasion, he was buying a horse when three or four friendly neighbors were present. He galloped the animal a short distance, and announced that he proposed to shoot the two top wires on a fence about thirty yards away. He wheeled sidewise, brought up his gun and fired two quick shots, cutting the top and second wires halfway between the posts. "I could do the trick about once in three times," he confessed, in *Thrilling Events*,[16] "and killing the coyote and rabbit at such distances were only scratch shots. But all this reached the officers' ears with exaggeration common to such stories, and made me a truly bogy-man to the best of them."

During that winter he attended a number of country dances: "People for miles around had known me since I was a child and gave me a hearty welcome; and while I danced, a couple of volunteers would stand guard outside to warn me of any danger. I was like all young men— flattered by the attention shown me by the pretty girls, and never missed a chance to be in their company. But for three years I'd had May Morrison for my sweetheart. She had grown into a young lady, believing the good in me and rejecting the bad. Her parents made no objection to my calling on her still, and the country round, including the marshals, knew I was courting her. Despite the close watch kept for me, I managed to call every week or two. I make mention of her because she played a very important part in my career, as you shall see. I shall not rave about her, as we are always daffy over our first love, but it might not be amiss to say that she was a beauty, of

44

Irish-Welsh descent, with auburn hair that curled naturally, large hazel eyes and a fair complexion. I might add that she was as good as she was beautiful.

"My friends urged me to leave the Indian Territory, and I decided to get a good sum of money and beat it. So in March, '93, I broached the subject of robbing a bank to Frank Cheney, and found he was willing. . . ." [17]

V

–Then to the Banks

For months, Starr had scouted the Big Caney river country around Bartlesville. It was only natural that he should choose the bank at Caney, Kansas, a prosperous little community of one thousand, in the southwest corner of Montgomery County and about two miles above the Indian Territory border.

They started north at once, Cheney riding a fine racing mare, Starr on a well-bred horse of speed and endurance. In the vicinity of Nowata they stopped for a few days and bought two extra horses, common cow ponies, on which to make their first run. They concealed their good horses about twenty miles below the border, and the day before their venture rode to a friend's house nearby and spent the night.

"Of course, we did not tell him our plans," Starr wrote.[1] "There were two ladies in the family, and we invited a

46

couple of other families in to dance. This lasted until 3 A.M., and after a few hours' sleep and a late breakfast, we saddled and started to Caney. . . ."

The date was March 27.

"Our idea was to ride slow and arrive in town about 3 P.M. We each carried two Winchesters and two revolvers, more than our accustomed amount of arms; but we thought that in such a big venture the extra ones might come in handy. We planned to conceal our rifles about two miles from town . . . felt that we would be able to do the bank and get to the street before the alarm was given, then a few more seconds would bring us to our horses, and if there was any shooting, we could give a pretty fair showing with our pistols. Just as we were hiding our rifles, a light shower fell, making the ground a little slippery. I knew the town well and hitched about fifty yards from the bank on a back street. I looked at Frank to see if he showed any signs of 'cold-feet,' but his jaw was set and his blue eyes glowed with determination. We separated and reached the front of the Caney Valley Bank at the same time. . . ."

The (Caney) Daily *Chronicle,* of March 28, 1893, reported the details:

The man that entered first at once proceeded to obtain command of the situation. The only persons in the bank were Cashier F. S. Hollingsworth, Clerk Harry Scurr and M. McEniry, vice-president of the First National Bank of Coffeyville.

As they entered one of the men proceeded toward the back room or council room. Cashier Hollingsworth, looking up, spoke, saying, "How do you do." The robber

47

merely nodded and replied, "How d'do," and passed
on as if looking for someone. Hollingsworth turned and
looked after him, thinking he would tell him there was
no one there. Just then something attracted his attention
in the front of the bank, when he discovered the other
man standing right in front of him with two six-shooters
pointing at his face, saying, "That's all right, hold up
your thumbs." Meantime young Cass Todd had entered
the bank, pushing in front of the last robber, and not
noticing anything wrong or unusual, stepped up to the
change window, laid down a check book, and stood
leaning against the counter expecting to make a de-
posit of $75, which was folded in bills between the
leaves of his check book. At this junction the robber who
had passed into the council room found Judge McEniry,
who thinking it was some drunken man making a play
with his pistol, retired into the private room back of the
vault, where the robber followed him and forced him
out again and into the business room, where Cashier
Hollingsworth and Clerk Scurr were.

Now the robber who had been standing in the outer
room behind the counter turned his weapon on young
Todd and forced him to throw up his hands and go
before him around through the council room and into
the business apartment, where he made all those present
stand in the corner at the west side in front of the vault.
The one who had cornered Judge McEniry found in
the private room a Winchester belonging to the bank,
and had reinforced himself with the weapon and now
came to the exchange window near where Hollingsworth was standing, and seeing two revolvers hanging
under the counter reached and took possession of them

48

and said to the cashier: "What do you keep these things for? Don't you know you can't use them?"

All this had been so quietly done and so quickly that those in the bank had hardly time to realize the situation.

At this juncture another citizen walked unsuspectingly into the jaws of peril. This was Enos Parsons, who says: "The first thing I saw was a man pointing a weapon at me and saying, 'Walk right in, pass right back this way; you won't be hurt if you behave yourself.'" He says at first he thought it was merely some young man having a little fun, and he merely looked up and grinned. But the fellow says, "B- G-- I mean it!" and then Parsons looked around and saw the others standing with hands up and he concluded something was up and he instantly obeyed, passing around through the council room and took his place with the rest and put up his hands.

Then followed two other citizens, Len Peterson, and after him Stephen Sanders, both of whom were disposed of in the same way that Parsons and Todd had been. This took some little time, perhaps five minutes, none of them having time to realize what was going on until the act was accomplished and the robbers were in possession of the loose money, and had emptied the contents of the vault into their sack.

They then proceeded to make the seven men go out of the building into the high enclosure at the rear of the bank, and cautioned them to keep quiet.

They then locked the back door and ran out the front way and turned on a trot down State Street, toward their horses.

As they were making their way toward their horses, the little man carried the money, which was quite a load, and the taller one covered the rear with the Winchester.

Just across the street were three men passing up from Burris' livery stable. These were Mr. Shinn, Geo. Garlinghouse and Harry Dunn.

He, the man with the Winchester, called to these men to hold up their thumbs. They did not understand the import of the first call, and he called to them in louder tones: "Hold up your thumbs." Even then they paid little attention to him, thinking he was merely some fellow amusing himself. But when he called out to them the third time and raised his Winchester to his face, they began to realize that something was wrong, and Mr. Shinn dodged in at Henderson's and the other two passed around the corner.

By this time the men who had been cooped up like rats in the back yard of the bank managed to break through the fence at the west side and running around to the front raised the alarm.

Then there was such hurrying and scurrying as has not been seen this side of Gotham since the surrender of the Dutch at New Amsterdam. Men rushed hither and yon, everybody calling everybody else to do something and nobody doing anything.

The robbers quietly got on their horses . . . and rode off.

They went out of town the same way they came in, and did not seem in the least hurried or flurried. The only person who made any effort to follow in a reasonable length of time was Ed Pearce, our young marshal, who immediately mounted and followed them at the distance of perhaps half a mile. Meanwhile great crowds of curious gazers and gawpers had gathered at the bank and on the corners, and the yawpers were foremost in the crowd and each telling what he would, might or could have done if only he had been there. Three quarters of an hour had elapsed before any organized effort was made to pursue the robbers or reinforce the young marshal. . . .

Finally, some system was organized out of all the confusion and a fine and able posse started out. . . . No results however are reported from the chase. The riders all returned in the evening and it was then an assured fact which must pass into history that Caney had a genuine bank robbery by real live robbers and the robbers had ridden away in broad daylight, and carried with them whole skins and a goodly weight of boodle. . . . Various rumors concerning the amount of the loss sustained by the bank were set afloat but at this writing we have reasonable assurance from the officials that the amount of the "crack" was not over two thousand dollars, or twenty-five hundred at the fartherest. . . .

Starr's version is almost identical to the *Chronicle*'s, except for the amount of loot taken:

"When we reached the outskirts of town, we rode faster and were soon to where our Winchesters were hidden. We threw away the one we had brought from the bank, first bending the barrel over a fence. We went over the hill south and turned due east. Our pursuers thought we had made for the Osage hills and went southwest. We got to our relay mounts long before night, ate our supper and started southeast. At dawn, we unsaddled at a friend's house, ninety miles from Caney. I was not very tired, so we counted our haul before breakfast. Frank had come out of the vault with his sack two-thirds full of greenbacks; didn't even bother to take the silver. Although the bills made a roll big enough to choke a hippopotamus, to our surprise and chagrin, it counted up to only $4,900. The foxy cashier had outmanaged us; we learned afterwards that while we were taming the crowd he had thrown all the bills of large denomination, amounting to $16,000, behind a pile of ledgers." [2]

Starr had a great deal of satisfaction, however, from the comments in the *Chronicle:*

> It would appear from a casual survey of the features of the case that the Daltons have been outdone altogether. . . . For coolness, smoothness and daring this adventure has not perhaps its equal in the history of the state . . . not been equaled in this intensely interesting line of human activity since the days of the Youngers and Jameses. . . .
>
> At least twenty-five men were within calling distance of the bank, and yet not a single person knew what was going on until the robbers were on their horses and riding out of the city. Not a single shot was fired, not a drop of blood spilled. The two men were doubtless experts, and to this fact we owe the remarkable good health of all our citizens. . . .

•

Stephen Sanders says he didn't catch on until he saw one of the men shoulder the sack.

Cass Todd says he did not feel the least bit tired from holding up his hands.

•

Enos Parsons says, "Them fellers meant it, you bet."

•

Wasn't that coolness?

•

A perfect walk away.

•

Wasn't it easy?

•

Who got the boodle? Boodle! Boodle, boodle. . . .

Starr was never arrested nor indicted for the Caney robbery, but it was common knowledge that he had engineered it, and an additional $1,700 reward was placed on his head. His easy success caused several badmen to want to join him, and he was so "completely enthralled" by the excitement of the game by this time that, by the end of April, he had organized as desperate a band of bank-and-train bandits as ever infested the Indian Territory.

He listed the members as follows: [3]

53

Hank Watt, about 35, sallow complexion, blue eyes and dark hair, well-educated, deadly with a rifle or six-shooter, and game to the core.

Bud Tyler, 30 years old, dark complexion and fierce-looking, but a little gun-shy.

Link Cumplin, about 30, light hair and blue eyes; a game man, but somewhat chicken-hearted.

Happy Jack (so-called because of his dolorous visage), about 27, dark hair and eyes; a square fellow and full of sand.

Kid Wilson (no relation to the slain marshal), a deadly, smooth-faced youth of 19, 5 feet 4 inches in height, brown hair and eyes; willing to take a chance, but too hot-headed.

All except Wilson had spent most of their lives in the Nations. Of his antecedents nothing is known. The only time he ever spoke of relatives, he said: "They have never done anything to place me where I am; they live on the other side of the globe and I prefer to say nothing of them." [4]

Frank Cheney was a Texan by birth, but had been reared in Colorado and New Mexico. He was 35, sandy-haired and blue-eyed, daring to the point of recklessness, an excellent shot and somewhat of a wit. The gang assembled on his farm near Wagoner, where Starr planned the next big job of his career.

"To show our contempt for the dinky deputy marshals, we fitted out a chuck and ammunition wagon, and as Tyler was the weakest at arms, we made him teamster. After leaving Cheney's we proceeded to Pryor Creek, and on the 2nd of May, six of us went in to rob the train. . . ." [5]

The Fort Smith *Weekly Elevator,* of Friday, May 5, 1893, tells how this was done:

The southbound passenger train on the M. K. & T. was held up at Pryor Creek Tuesday night by six men, who went through the smoker and two passenger cars, relieving the passengers of what money they had but doing no act of violence except to strike the telegraph operator of the station on the head with a revolver for attempting to manipulate the keys of his instrument.

From C. D. Reeves, of Kansas City, we gather particulars. The train, which was due at 8 o'clock, did not arrive until 8:10. No sooner had it stopped than the robbers began a fusillade with Winchesters, their shots being fired, apparently, in the air, without intent to injure anyone. The engineer was covered by a Winchester in the hands of one of the outlaws, and a break was made for the express car. The door of this car was locked, but the robbers effected an entrance by breaking a panel of the door. A number of shots were exchanged between them and the messenger, but no injury was inflicted. The messenger was finally compelled to come on the outside. The robbers made a desperate attempt to get into the safe, but failed to do so and nothing was taken from there. The messenger was treated pretty roughly. He was thrown to the ground and a number of shots fired at or in such close proximity to him as to make him feel decidedly uncomfortable.

The outlaws first went through the smoker. They then entered the passenger cars. One man stood near the front door with a Winchester, while another collected the "fares." Nothing was taken from the ladies or any of the male passengers who had the appearance of being working men. Money seemed to be the sole object of search. Watches and jewelry were ignored. Two watches were taken but both returned to their owners. As each passenger was reached he was asked to "put up" what he had about him, which of course he did without much demurring, as the gaping barrel of the Winchester had a very persuasive effect. Mr. Reeves had about $200 on his person, also a diamond scarf-pin. As soon as the firing began he took in the situation and taking $10 from his roll of bills put it in his pocket. The remainder he hid in his shirt-bosom. His diamond pin he thrust into his hat lining. When his turn came he handed Mr. Robber his ten dollar bill and what silver he had, remarking that he hoped enough would be left to carry him to Fort Smith. His despoiler at once returned $2.50, remarking, "The fare to Fort Smith is $2.45, take it." One old gentleman who sat back of Mr. Reeves and who was well fixed so far as world's goods are concerned, got off because it was noticed, as he went to hand out his pile, that the palms of his hands were calloused and he had the appearance of a hard-working farmer. Mr. Reeves is of a jocular disposition, and while he was undergoing the process of being robbed asked the man with the Winchester if he had anything that would cure a sore eye. (One of Mr. Reeves' eyes is inflamed and he wears a protector over it.) The response was: "No, but I've got something that can make the other one d----d sore." Mr. Reeves concluded that the fellow was in no mood for joking and made no further inquiries.

The sleeper was not entered. The conductor, upon being asked if anybody was in that car, said that it was a dead-head car, with nobody in it. Right here the robbers missed a haul, for the sleeper contained a party of Kansas City capitalists, each of whom, it is to be presumed, had a good roll of money with him.

One unfortunate fellow, a drummer, who had been in the town selling goods, came into the train while the robbers were at work. He was utterly unconscious of danger until he stepped aboard, when he was ordered to "put up." He lost $185.

The outlaws made no attempt at concealment, not even wearing masks. . . . The man who stood in the front corner of the car with a Winchester leveled at the passengers is five feet and six inches in height, rather sparely made, pale blue or gray eyes, complexion rather sandy-looking, having the appearance of being red-headed [Cheney]. . . . The man who collected the "fares" is about five feet six inches in height; short, stocky build; full-faced from cheek bones down; will weigh 175 or 180 pounds; had a blue double-breasted sack coat which he wore unbuttoned [Wilson]. One of the others is about six feet in height; has prominent cheek bones, and will weigh 190 or 200 pounds. Has the appearance in complexion and color of eyes [black] to be about one-eighth Indian [Starr]. . . .

The Vinita *Indian Chieftain,* of May 4, 1893, adds one important item:

. . . The [express] car being entered, the safes were ordered opened but the messenger protested that he could not unlock the "through" safe and finally satisfied the robbers of that fact. The "local" safe was quickly opened and yielded up a quantity of jewelry and some lottery tickets. Attention was then directed to robbing such persons as were captured about the depot and then the passengers, as far back as the sleeper. When the work was completed the robbers marched their victims down the track to where six horses were tied, mounted and rode off. . . .

"We realized $6,000 and a consignment of unset diamonds," Starr said,[6] "and no one was hurt, although we did a lot of firing as a means of intimidation.

"After the robbery we rode some twenty miles and established camp. The next day we crossed the Frisco and Missouri-Pacific railroads and made our way leisurely to the vicinity of Nowata. Although we knew that our doings had been telegraphed everywhere, we did not try to hide; rather, for sheer hellishness, we decided to give our farmer friends a free daylight exhibition of nerve.

"We all were superbly mounted on well-bred horses and cowboy saddles. We wore spurs and each man carried a Winchester of large caliber, Model '86, and two Colts in fine wide leather belts. Instead of forming a line like the cavalry, we formed fanshape, each man on the outside was to begin shooting always at the extreme right or left, and the center to center; this was done to keep two or more from firing at the same target, if attacked. We were shooting at least a hundred bullets a day each to keep in trim, and our expenses per day, not including our ammunition and clothes, were $30, or $10 for each meal, and we had every delicacy to be obtained. I don't believe an outlaw camp was ever conducted along the same line as ours. The railroad offered $1,200 for me, dead or alive, and the Pryor Creek trainmen $1,000, making $2,200 for this trick alone. Still we made no effort to conceal ourselves. . . ."

On May 3, a telegram was received by Marshal Yoes at Fort Smith, from Nowata: "Starr and five men here tonight. Send enough men to arrest them."[7] Not an officer showed.

"Well, we went through our maneuvers," Starr said,[8] "and frightened the whole neighborhood out of its wits. We boasted everywhere we stopped that we could whip all the deputies on the force. These same deputies were willing to arrest innocent and harmless boys and drag them off to jail, and with the fees thus gained drink Fort Smith whiskey and pose as heroes before the demimonde; but they wouldn't risk their immoral hides in an attempt to arrest real violators of the law, though some of them were regarded as man-killers."

His vanity running high, Henry turned his outfit down the Verdigris. They turned east at Sequoyah, passing back through the Pryor Creek country, forded the Grand River, and crossed the Cherokee border into northwestern Arkansas. By the first of June they were camped within sixteen miles of Bentonville, a little community of two thousand, which, shortly after the Civil War, had been made famous by the James boys' raiding and the looting of Craig & Son's store.

Henry wasn't interested in duplicating the feat of the Jameses—Bentonville was the county seat and a rich town, and its People's Bank was one of the healthiest institutions of its kind in that part of the country. He rode in to case the place alone. When he returned, he knew the habits of all its employees, the location of every street, alley, store, house, and vacant lot. There was a small difficulty: the sixteen miles between camp and town was across an open valley thickly settled.

"We hired a buggy in Bentonville the night before the robbery to transport our rifles across this farming district without attracting attention," Starr wrote.[9] "The date was June 5, '93. At 11:30 A.M., we started, aiming to make the sixteen miles in three hours. Cheney and I rode in the buggy and led our horses. The other four boys rode two and two about a mile apart. As we neared town we closed up and all got to a back street at the same time. . . ."

Starr and Cheney drove around the courthouse square into the alley behind the office of the Bentonville *Sun*. It was 2:30 P.M. Quickly, the others followed and dismounted. Happy Jack held the reins of the six saddled horses while the rest snatched their rifles from under a blanket in the rear of the buggy and dog-trotted single file a half block north to the bank. Watt posted himself where he could cover the escape route to the horses. Cumplin was left on guard at the bank door. The door was open, and Starr darted inside, Cheney and Kid Wilson at his heels. They prodded four surprised bank officials (President A. W. Dinsmore, Vice President I. R. Hull, Cashier J. H. McAndrew, and Assistant Cashier George B. Jackson) and two customers against the wall with the usual salutation "Thumbs up and stand steady," and proceeded to get the cash.

Wilson leaped behind the counter. Cheney went inside the vault. Within five minutes, they had all the loose money stuffed in two sacks—one containing $11,000 in gold and currency, the other $900 in silver—and were ready to go.

It had been time enough, however, for the people to realize their bank was being robbed. As the alarm spread, citizens seized rifles and shotguns and opened fire on Watt and Cumplin.

A tousle-headed kid scampered to the courthouse like a frightened jackrabbit. He found Sheriff Pierce Galbraith in the county judge's office. "They're holding up the bank!" he yelled. The sheriff grabbed his Winchester and ran to where he could see the robbers' horses in the alley.

Cumplin, who was walking back and forth below the bank, was getting it from all sides. Four or five men were shooting at him from across the street—and hitting him— with shotguns loaded with buckshot. When he tried to move down toward the horses, two men tried to pepper him from across the square. Happy Jack was dancing a jig, trying to hold the horses and dodge the bullets from Sheriff Galbraith's rifle.

Inside the bank, Starr took the sack of gold and currency and handed the sack of silver to Assistant Cashier Jackson, giving Wilson and Cheney free hands with their Winchesters. He ordered the other captives to leave the bank first, intending to use them as a screen. But once outside, with a dozen citizens shooting at them, it was no more dangerous not to stay with the robbers, and they scattered like quail in every direction. The robbers let them go and continued their march down South Main Street with Jackson still in front of them. The cashier was wounded in the back of the head and left elbow as they forced him along the sidewalk.

Then the unforeseen occurred. A courageous young lady, employed as business manager in the office of the Bentonville *Sun,* saved his life. As Jackson, still carrying the sack of silver, passed the office, Miss Maggie Wood reached outside, seized him by the shoulders and jerked him bodily into the room. Before the robbers recovered from surprise, she closed and locked the door.

There was no time to try to recover the silver. The gunfire in the street had increased. The robbers' guns blazed. They drove Clint Croxdale back inside his drug store. Taylor Stone, a farmer, who was standing by the side of Craig's store taking aim with a shotgun, fell with a shot through the left groin and hip. He dragged himself back

61

around the corner into the Wood and Hamel barbershop. Tom Baker, another farmer, was shot in the chin, and returned the compliment by putting a bullet through the right arm of Link Cumplin.

Cumplin was no longer able to use his rifle. He was a "mass of wounds, one of them in the eyes, and had to be assisted in mounting." Starr and Cheney were the last to reach their horses. Then all mounted and tore out of town to the west, with lead volleying after them and Sheriff Galbraith and an angry posse in pursuit.[10]

VI

Capture at Colorado Springs

For fifteen miles the posse followed them, never "within range" but "just dogging" at their heels.[1] Jim Craig [2] states that at the Lark Wilson farm four miles west of town, the robbers took a horse from a man named Lee McAllister; the delay brought the posse close enough to open fire on them, "driving them off without scoring a hit"; and a few miles further, they "forced a boy to trade horses with them, leaving him a very tired animal." With no telegraph or telephones available, Galbraith sent part of his posse across country to "cut them off," but the bandits, "thinking ahead also, left the road in time to avoid the sheriff's trap."

At Decatur, they met the Siloam Springs stage en route to Bentonville, and Starr sent a warning to the sheriff that he would die if he persisted in the pursuit: "True to our word, about a mile further, Frank, Kid and I doubled back on his flank and killed seven of their horses. The sheriff gave up the chase and went back to Bentonville." [3]

Craig says only one horse was lost in this skirmish and that the posse turned back because of approaching darkness. Too, they were concerned about what was going on in Bentonville and their friends who had been injured. The next day everyone came to town to learn the details of the holdup. President W. R. McIlroy and Cashier J. L. Dickson, of the bank at Fayetteville, arrived by train with $8,000 cash to meet the emergency until more money could be obtained from the bank in St. Louis. The loss totaled $11,001.53. To the people of Benton County, this was the "only big robbery there ever was," and for years afterwards, it was the topic of conversation when old timers got together. [4]

Starr and his men rode all night, and about 3 P.M. the next day reached Cheney's farm near Wagoner. They divided the loot and decided to split up for a while. But the territory got so hot they never united. Happy Jack was shot from ambush in the Cherokee Nation two months later; Watt was killed in a battle with officers in 1895; Link Cumplin died of his wounds the same year, in Alaska; Tyler died in bed of "natural causes" in 1908.

Cheney rode northwest with Starr and Wilson, leaving them after a two-day rest at a friend's house on the Verdigris. Starr describes the parting: [5] "Neither [of us] mentioned that we ever expected to see each other again. Our friendship was too genuine for any theatricals, so we shook hands quickly. Frank sprang on his horse and headed south to the Creek country. As I reached the top of a hill, I saw Frank riding in a flat some distance away. The day was partly cloudy. Just as he reached the edge of some timber, the sun came out bright and his white shirt and the flaxen mane and tail of his thoroughbred horse flashed in the sunlight. I was for a moment overcome with a feeling of inexpressible sadness as he wheeled to wave his last adieu and disappeared. May his brave soul rest in peace and the traitors who caused his death in eternal damnation...."

Cheney supposedly spent the next few months of his life in South America. But he was back in the Cherokee country by the early spring of 1894. He robbed a store at Fort Gibson, shot and killed Officer Bill Cain at Nelson, on the Middle Boggy River, Choctaw Nation, to escape arrest, and fled to Texas. In Collin County, he teamed up with John Keegan, wanted for murder at Caddo, and robbed the bank at Plano. Next, they held up the station agent at Sanger, in Denton County, stole a double-seated phaeton and some horses, and started east to rob the Red River County bank at Clarksville. They crossed Red River into the Choctaw Nation, recrossed into Texas near the mouth of the Boggy, traveled down the river to Slate Shoals, a little village in the extreme northeast corner of Lamar County, then crossed back into the Indian Territory in an effort to "tangle their trail." Their actions aroused the suspicions of Deputy United States Marshals Joe McKee, D. E. Booker and Lee McAfee, of Paris, who procured a hack and followed them. On the morning of July 13, the officers, with possemen Dave Wilson, Jim Jackson, and John Lewis, overtook them near Eagletown. They hid in some heavy undergrowth bordering the narrow roadway and waited. The robbers "drove into the ambuscade without any suspicion of danger ... until ordered to hold up their hands. Instinctively they reached for their guns ... a volley from Winchesters and shotguns rang out and the two men in the phaeton fell to the ground, riddled with bullets and buckshot." [6]

After parting with Cheney, Starr tried to see May Morrison again, but found the country "swarming with catchpoles." Grover Cleveland had returned to the White House as President. On May 29, 1893, he had named George J. Crump to replace Jacob Yoes as chief marshal at Fort Smith. A manhunter of no mean reputation, Crump considered the capture of Starr his personal responsibility. He had led twelve deputies into the Nowata area, and ordered a like number into the Verdigris and Big Caney countries. His movement was backed by special officers from Wells-Fargo and other express companies, who were searching the Cherokee Nation from Pryor Creek to Coffeyville. [7]

Starr and Wilson remained in hiding near the friend's house on the Verdigris: "We selected a deep ravine where three large oak trees grew—a fine place to put up a defense. The next day at 2 o'clock we saw sixteen horsemen a couple of miles away, who were apparently following our trail. We had plenty of time to have made a good getaway, as our horses had rested fourteen hours, and theirs were jaded . . . but thought the two of us under these conditions would be a match for the whole sixteen, which proves that we were at least not much afraid.

"They dismounted at our friend's house, got a drink and inquired if he had seen us. He told them he had seen us riding north early that morning. The marshals knew he was lying, as they had trailed our shod horses in the soft ground to the very door, and also knew we were in the river bottoms only a half mile east; they rode north. We had spread a blanket on the ground with about a hundred loose cartridges on it, so that we could grab them quick in case of an attack. It would have been no battle—but slaughter. From our vantage point behind the big trees we could have mowed them down without exposure. . . . We stayed in our location until night, then got safely away from the authorities." [8]

Within a few days, Starr met his sweetheart by appointment in the Osage, and in a covered wagon, with Kid Wilson as bodyguard, they drove to Emporia, Kansas:

"In deference to the virtue and memory of Miss Morrison, and to put to rout a coterie of gossipers concerning her, the reason I didn't marry her in Indian Territory is evident to anyone, and I did intend to and would have married her as soon as effectually away. Our intention was to catch a fast train to California and go from there to Old Mexico. However, we stopped at Colorado Springs to replenish the lady's wardrobe. . . ." [9]

Starr, 17-year-old May Morrison, and Kid Wilson arrived in Colorado Springs, Colorado, late Saturday night, July, 1, 1893. Going to the Spaulding House, a medium-priced but reputable hotel, they registered as Frank Jackson, Mary Jackson, and John Wilson—all of Joplin, Missouri. The events that transpired in the next twenty-four hours are gathered from the Fort Smith *Weekly Elevator,* of Friday, July 7: [10]

Monday morning, July 3, William Feuerstine, a Fort Smith merchant, who was in the resort city on private business and living at the Spaulding House, stepped into the dining room and recognized the man to whom he had sold goods from his store following his release from the federal jail in 1892. He could not allow Starr an opportunity of recognizing him. He hastened back to his room, summoned clerk Byron Himebaugh, and requested him to notify Colorado Springs' chief of police, L. C. Dana.

Chief Dana, a veteran police officer, inwardly discounted the report as a false alarm, but he treated the jittery clerk politely and went to the hotel to investigate, alone. After a long, close look at the men in the dining room, and their female companion, Dana was convinced.

Well aware of the desperate character of the pair, he decided to keep them under surveillance until such time as they could be approached separately. Four officers, heavily armed, were posted in a convenient room on South Tejon Street to watch the hotel. Detective Joe Atkinson was detailed at the Spaulding House to "keep the game in sight."

Shortly after noon, Starr and Wilson sauntered up Tejon Street to Huerfano Avenue, and entered the Oppenheim Brothers store. They purchased fine new four-button suits and bowler hats, gold watches and chains to match, and expressed a desire to see the sights of the neighborhood. The Oppenheims provided a carriage, and two members of the firm agreed to accompany them. "Mrs. Jackson" was taken on at the Spaulding House, and the party drove to Manitou, where they spent the rest of the day. Detectives watched their every move.

They returned at dark. Starr and the woman got out at the Spaulding House; Wilson accompanied the rig to the stable. An hour later, Starr descended to the hotel office. On being informed that the supper hour had passed, he again walked up Tejon Street to Huerfano and entered the Cafe Royal.

This was the moment anxiously waited for—the desperadoes had separated. Chief Dana and Captain J. W. Gathright leisurely strode into the cafe. Starr was occupied with his meal. The officers walked past his table. Turning suddenly, they pinioned his arms and wrists. Then Detective Atkinson and his men rushed in, covering him with their six-shooters and relieving him of the .45 Colt's revolver concealed under his coat.

"I had made up my mind to fight to the end, irrespective of time, location or odds," Starr wrote, in *Thrilling Events*.[11] "I had pledged myself that I would not be caught until I had fired my last shot, whether it was on the open prairies of the Indian Territory or the crowded streets of a big city. But, touch a man's vanity and you are sure to touch a tender spot, and I admit that this time I was completely whipped without getting a scratch. I, who had made the gun-fighting marshals of the territories stand back—I, the 'Bear-Cat' of a bunch of sure bad hombres—had been arrested, without a shot being fired, by five pot-bellied policemen!"

He was taken to headquarters. "Who do you think you've got?" he asked.

"Henry Starr," Dana replied.

Starr smiled. "It is a good thing you jumped me from behind or there would have been some corpses around," he observed mildly.

Meanwhile, Kid Wilson had taken a street car to Colorado City and entered a house of ill fame. Another detective squad was soon in pursuit. When the landlady opened the door to the room, the officers rushed in, ordering him to throw up his hands. Wilson offered no resistance. He was lying in bed with his revolver under his pillow.

With the two men in jail, Dana and Gathright went to the Spaulding House and awoke "Mrs. Jackson." Under her pillow they found $1600 in greenbacks and a .38 pearl-handled revolver. In a valise nearby was $500 in gold.

She told conflicting stories at first of her relationship with Starr and about the money. She said her name was Mary Jones and that her parents lived in Joplin; there she had met "Frank Jackson," who professed to be a well-to-do Texas cattleman, and married him after a whirlwind courtship. She almost fainted when Chief Dana informed her that Starr and Wilson were in custody. Finally, she admitted her identity.

The news of Starr's arrest spread quickly. At Fort Smith, Marshal Crump wired for verification. Chief Dana wired back: "No doubt about it. Both he and his wife admit it, and $2100 found on his person."

Crump immediately forwarded the necessary papers to hold Starr for murder and Wilson for complicity in the Pryor Creek and Bentonville robberies. On July 5, they were transferred to the custody of the United States marshal at Denver. The girl was released to return to her home in the Indian Territory. A few days later, heavily manacled and chained and accompanied by Deputy Marshals Brown and William C. Smith, Starr and Wilson boarded the 8 o'clock train to Fort Smith, Arkansas, via Kansas City and Springfield.

All along the line, newspapers carried the story of their capture. The Kansas City *Star* termed it "a change in the bank and train robber business"; claimed that "the time has passed when such outlaws can venture safely into towns, relying either on the assistance of friends, or the cowardice or carelessness of officers"; and suggested: "A little more of the revival of common courage all around, and such men will cease to exist as a special class of malefactors."

"The sensational correspondents worked overtime," said Starr.[12] "Mine and Wilson's pictures were on the front pages of all the big dailies, but the prize lie of the aggregation ran thus: That the young lady with me was the daughter of a wealthy Eastern family, and that while robbing a train I had been struck with her beauty and taken her by force to an outlaw retreat, while she in turn had fallen in love with me. The St. Louis *Republic* in particular printed trash unreadable about her and the gapings of the crowds sure made me sore."

According to the Oklahoma City *Times*, of September 19, 1913: "At the time of the Katy train robbery at Pryor Creek, August, 1892 [*sic*] . . . Starr remained on the platform of the first coach while his men were getting the available cash. While he was standing there a girl wild with terror jumped off and disappeared in the darkness. The train was delayed but about half an hour by the bandits and at the end of that time Starr and his men, on horseback, rode off through the woods. When some distance from the railroad they found the girl, who seemed crazed with fear. Starr recognized her as the girl who jumped from the train. He took her on his horse to the camp of the outlaws. The young lady said her home was in Joplin, Mo. She learned to like the bandit leader. After several days she was taken to a railroad station and went to her home. Before starting, however, Starr, it is said, told the girl that he would come to Joplin and visit her. He did, under an assumed name, and they were married."

Similar imaginative pieces appeared in the *Illustrated Buffalo Express* of October, 1913, and the Tulsa *World* of March 29, 1915, and the story has been repeated by careless writers ever since.

At Monett, Missouri, the prisoners were met by Marshal Crump, with a strong force of deputies, and Sheriff Galbraith of Bentonville. "This weazened-faced sheriff made himself obnoxious by asking foolish questions," Starr wrote,[13] "and I finally told him that a man of my reputation and dignity could not afford to hold conversation with a backwoods county officer. This was horse-play to get rid of him, of course, but it created a laugh.

"An immense crowd was at the Fort Smith depot to see us come in. It was July 13. Photographers and reporters galore were at every vantage point. The newspapers and local sentiment were very strong against me. This was not strange as Floyd Wilson, the man I killed near Nowata, had lived in Fort Smith for years, and his widow still lived there. I had about as much show for justice as a lone sheep in the midst of a pack of gray wolves.

"I employed as council the Honorable W. H. H. Clayton, Colonel William M. Cravens and Judge Thomas Barnes, all noted criminal lawyers. Messrs. Clayton and Barnes had each served as district attorney for the government. Despite the hostile feeling and prejudice, these men, true to their professional honor, began a fight for me with a zeal and skill remarkable even in that infamous criminal court."

VII

Henry Starr and the "Hanging Judge"

Sheriff Galbraith and Assistant Cashier Jackson identified Starr and Wilson as members of the gang that had robbed the bank at Bentonville. Both were indicted for the crime in Benton County, but the officials there saw no hope, at least temporarily, of returning the pair for trial in the face of the numerous federal indictments that followed rapidly. As Starr put it, "Uncle Sam had a murder charge and eight or ten cases of highway robbery against me, and the state of Arkansas had to wait." [1] Starr's mother and sister tried to get him out on bond, without success. [2]

The People's Bank filed suit against Starr in the United States court for the $11,000 stolen from the institution. He denied having received any money from the bank, and asked that the bank be made to prove its claims. Judgment by default was taken against him for $11,001, with interest, and an attachment issued against the $2,200 found in his possession at Colorado Springs.[3] Mrs. Floyd Wilson also sued for $10,000 damages for the death of her husband, and another attachment was issued upon the money taken from Starr when arrested. Nothing ever came of it, however, and the judgment in favor of the Bentonville bank finally was set aside because at the time it was obtained Starr was under indictment for the Pryor Creek train robbery, the robbery of Shufeldt's store at Lenapah and Carter's store at Sequoyah, and not represented in court.[4] Milo Creekmore, who had surrendered to federal officers in March, was indicted with him in the two store robberies.[5] On August 10, Starr was arraigned in court for the murder of Floyd Wilson. He pleaded not guilty. His trial was set for October 16.

Starr and Wilson apparently saw little use in staying around to defend themselves, and determined, if possible, to "again breathe the air of freedom." The St. Louis *Republic* of October 3, reported:

[They] led an unsuccessful attempt to break jail . . . assisted by John Pointer, Alexander Allen and Frank Collins, condemned murderers, and Charles Young and Jim Fair. They refused to go into their cells at dinner time and made an attack upon one of the guards, who tried to force them into their cells. One guard fired, shooting Young in the face and breaking the cheekbone, but not seriously injuring him. Pointer, Starr and Wilson begged to be shot."

The Fort Smith *Weekly Elevator*, of Friday, October 6, called it "A Mutiny":

Sunday morning about 11 o'clock the prisoners in two of the tiers of the Federal jail got together, and refused to go to their cells. . . . The ring-leaders in the affair were Henry Starr, Kid Wilson and John Pointer, the latter under sentence of death for murder. The cells in the jail are arranged in three tiers, one above the other. Those charged with murder are placed in the lower tier. Those charged with larceny and assaults are in the second, while the whiskey sellers are confined in the third or top tier.

A break was discovered in the floor of the third corridor one day last week, but it was not immediately repaired. Sunday morning it was enlarged so as to admit the prisoners to the second floor, the occupants of which took occasion to break through their floor into the corridor below. Marshal Crump tried to persuade the men to go back to their respective cells, but they refused to do so without a promise. They wanted to compromise. They were willing to retreat, but wanted to retreat with the honors of war. Marshal Crump informed them that his orders must be obeyed; that he preferred to hurt nobody, but would use what force was necessary to compel an observance of the rules; that unless they retired peaceably to their cells they would be forced in. Guards were then stationed in the corridors near the openings made by the prisoners with instructions to shoot any of the inmates of the upper tiers who should attempt to descend to the lower floor. The door of the lower corridor was opened and [Guard] Mont Baxter stepped in. As he did so, Charley Young, a negro convicted of larceny, advanced upon him, holding in each hand a large iron spittoon. Baxter thereupon ordered Young to halt, but upon the latter failing to do so, fired at him, the ball striking under the left eye and inflicting a severe though not fatal wound.

By this time the most desperate of the prisoners had armed themselves with spittoons, water jugs or whatever they could lay hands upon and advanced threateningly towards the door. This was closed, and Marshal Crump's patience having been exhausted, he took out his watch and told the excited men that if they were not back in their cells in five minutes his guards would commence firing. This had the desired effect, and before the time had expired every man was in his cell and locked up. . . . The ringleaders have since been punished by solitary confinement.

Matters worsened when Alf Cheney, a brother of Frank, was arrested by Deputy Marshal Heck Bruner at Wagoner on a warrant charging him with complicity in the Missouri-Kansas-Texas train robbery. Alf maintained that it was his brother the marshal wanted, but Bruner told him, "Both of you are wanted." [6] During the second week of October, Alf was convicted with Starr and Wilson of the holdup at Pryor Creek.

There were fifteen counts in the indictment. The jury found the prisoners guilty on six. There were a number of witnesses and nearly every one identified Starr and Wilson, "though only a few had seen Cheney well enough to say positively." Starr's and Wilson's attorneys early gave up hope of saving them, but fought hard to keep down the number of counts on which there should be a conviction. In an effort to clear Alf Cheney, Kid Wilson took the stand and declared the robbery had been committed by himself, Starr, Frank Cheney, and three others whom he knew only as Hank, Link, and Jack, but he failed to convince the jury.[7]

Commenting on the trial in *Thrilling Events,* Starr wrote:[8] "Alf Cheney's case is a fair instance of the brand of justice dealt out at Fort Smith in those days. Alf was at the depot at Wagoner, forty miles south of Pryor Creek, when the train that had been robbed there, and proved that fact by a score of reputable neighbors who had known him for years. . . . The only man that swore anything against him was the engineer, who testified that a man who might have been Alf came by the engine, but he really did not see him clearly. The district attorney argued that Alf could have assisted in the beginning of the robbery and then got a freight train into Wagoner ahead of the passenger train. A very weak and absurd contention. In an ordinary court of justice the jury would have acquitted him from the box. . . . Cheney's lawyer should have had a separate trial for him from Kid Wilson and I, whose reputations were of the worst. As the case proceeded I could see a conspiracy . . . and knowing that I would be convicted, and to save an innocent man, I told his attorney that I would go on the stand and acquit Cheney, but my offer was rejected. The cowardly pettifogger was in on the scheme to fix poor Cheney for a 'cut' of the $1,500 reward offered by the railroad and express companies. Cheney was given twenty-four years in the pen, ten of which he served. What the poor fellow must have suffered those ten long years is not pleasant to ponder."

Kid Wilson was given twenty-four years at Brooklyn, New York. Starr was not sentenced but immediately put on trial for looting the depot at Nowata and robbing the Schufeldt and Carter stores. Milo Creekmore acknowledged to the court that he was with Starr at Lenapah and Sequoyah, but denied being at Nowata. The Tahlequah *Cherokee Advocate*, of October 28, added this item: "Milo Creekmore was married to Miss Cora Runyon last Sunday at the residence of his mother in Fort Smith. After the ceremony and dinner served, he was taken back to jail, and the hopeful bride left to await the conclusion of the whole matter."

Starr was convicted on all three counts. "Of course I was guilty," he wrote,[9] "but the methods these people chose and the ease with which one cheap detective swore that I told him I did it—a lie all the way through—was something beyond belief. The traitor Creekmore turned state's evidence and went free. If ever a poor devil was a fall guy, it was I. Again I was not sentenced, then why spend time and expense convicting me on these highway cases?"

It was obvious to Starr that the prosecution was saving him for the rope. His trial for the murder of Floyd Wilson began as scheduled. The indictment, with an endorsement of witnesses, appears upon the court record in the following language:

UNITED STATES OF AMERICA,
Western District of Arkansas.

In the Circuit Court, August Term, A.D., 1893

UNITED STATES
vs.
Henry Starr
} Murder

The Grand Jurors of the United States of America, duly selected, empaneled, sworn and charged, to inquire in and for the body of the Western District of Arkansas aforesaid, upon their oath present:

That Henry Starr, on the 13th day of December A.D., 1892, at the Cherokee Nation, in the Indian Country, within the Western District of Arkansas aforesaid, with force and arms, in and upon the body of one Floyd Wilson, a white man and not an Indian, then and there being, feloniously, wilfully and of his malice aforethought, did make an assault; and that the said Henry Starr with a certain gun then and there charged with gunpowder and one leaden bullet, which said gun he the said Henry Starr in his hands then and there had and held, then and there feloniously, wilfully and of his malice aforethought, did discharge and shoot off, to, against and upon the said Floyd Wilson and that the said Henry Starr with the leaden bullet aforesaid, out of the gun aforesaid, then and there, by force of the gunpowder aforesaid, by the said Henry Starr discharged and shot off as aforesaid, then and there feloniously, wilfully and of his malice aforethought, did strike, penetrate and wound him the said Floyd Wilson in and upon the left side of the breast of him the said Floyd Wilson giving to him the said Floyd Wilson then and there, with the leaden bullet aforesaid, so as aforesaid discharged and shot out of the gun aforesaid by the said Henry Starr in and upon the left side of the breast of him the said Floyd Wilson one mortal wound of the depth of four inches and of the breadth of half an inch; of which said mortal wound, he the said Floyd Wilson then and there instantly died. And so the Jurors aforesaid, upon their oath aforesaid, do say that the said Henry Starr him

79

the said Floyd Wilson in the manner and by the means aforesaid, feloniously, wilfully and of his malice aforethought, did kill and murder, contrary to the form of the Statute in such cases made and provided, and against the peace and dignity of the United States of America.

I. W. Bruce, Foreman   Jas. F. Read
                              United States Attorney
                              Western District of Arkansas

Witnesses:

Arthur Dodge, 7 miles N. of Nowata, I. T.
Frank McGirl, 5 miles S. of Lenapah, I. T.
Emmett Miller, 8 miles S. of Lenapah, I. T.
Mary Patchett, 7 miles N. of Nowata, I. T.
Jno. T. Patchett, 7 miles N. of Nowata, I. T.
Henry C. Dickey, St. Louis, Mo.

Filed in open court August 8, 1893.

                         S. Wheeler, Clerk
                         by I. M. Dodge, Deputy Clerk[10]

Apparently Starr decided to change counsel. In this case he was defended by A. H. Garland, a famous Arkansas lawyer and politician since 1853. Garland had been a delegate to the first Confederate congress, and held a seat in the Senate when the Confederacy fell. In 1874, he had been elected governor of Arkansas, and in 1876, to the United States Senate, where he served until 1885, when he was appointed Attorney General in President Cleveland's first Cabinet.

"The proceedings would have been a joke were not a human life at stake," Starr said.[11] "The evidence was all in my favor and my attorney felt that manslaughter would be the severest verdict."

The chief witness for the prosecution was Detective Dickey. He told how he and Wilson were secreted at Arthur Dodge's ranch; Starr rode past and was quickly followed by Wilson on horseback; Dickey's horse was a wild one, bucked him off and then ran into a wire fence. Wilson finally began firing, and when he was down, Starr went up and "shot him dead," mounted his victim's horse and rode off.[12]

The other witnesses agreed that Wilson fired the first shot, and also that, during the time he was riding up on Starr, Starr did not raise his gun, or make any effort to stop Wilson. In response to questions by Assistant United States Attorney J. B. McDonough, they testified as follows:

ARTHUR DODGE:

Q. Did you know Floyd Wilson?
A. I never knew him until he came there in the night.
Q. When was that?
A. The second night before the killing . . . that would be the night of the 11th. Sunday night. . . . They [Dickey and Wilson] came there inquiring the road to Lipsy's. They came in, and I made a fire, and they warmed; it was a terrible cold, disagreeable night.
Q. Did they stay all night there?
A. No, sir; they went on to hunt Lipsy's. I told them how to get there the best I could.
Q. When did you next see them?

A. The next morning about the time we were getting ready for breakfast. . . .

Q. Did they eat breakfast at your house the next morning?

A. Yes, sir. . . .

Q. Did they inquire of you for Henry Starr?

A. Yes, sir . . . that night when they came there they said they understood he was at Lipsy's, and they were going there to find him.

Q. Had you seen Henry Starr that day?

A. It seems I did. . . . I will say this: I was in the habit of seeing him every day; he was constantly passing along, coming to the house there directly.

Q. Coming to your house?

A. Yes, sir. This Mary Patchett was cooking for me. . . . Her name at that time was Mary Black.

Q. Was she a friend of Starr's?

A. She seemed to be. . . .

Q. Was Henry Starr keeping company with her?

A. No, sir; he was just coming there occasionally, I think, to meet another young lady who would come there.

Q. Was the other young lady there at that time?

A. No, sir.

Q. Did you see Henry Starr during that day?

A. I didn't see him until about dark; just about the time we had lit the lamps, he came riding along . . . stopped at the gate and looked in at the house where they [the officers] were sitting . . . then turned and went out as straight south as he could. . . .

Q. Just commence where you first saw him and state it so it can be written down.

HENRY STARR
Last of the Real Badmen

A portfolio of album art, drawn from the extensive picture collection of the author, Oklahoma Historical Society, and University of Oklahoma Library, Division of Manuscripts.

Photo by J.L. Rivkin
© Tulsa 1919

Photo taken at Fort Smith, Arkansas, following Starr's capture at Colorado Springs, Colorado, July 3, 1893.

All photographs on this and the facing page are from author's collection.

"Kid" Wilson, member of Starr gang. Photo taken at Fort Smith, Arkansas, following his capture with Starr at Colorado Springs, July 3, 1893.

The old federal building with its basement jail at Fort Smith, Arkansas, where Henry Starr spent five years in prison pending appeals to the U. S. Supreme Court. He read much, wrote articles for newspapers about Indian Territory and Five Civilized Tribes.

Isaac Charles Parker, the "hanging judge" of Fort Smith, Arkansas, who twice sentenced Henry Starr to the gallows and was twice reversed by the United States Supreme Court.

AT RIGHT: John B. "Buck" McDonough, assistant U. S. Attorney at Fort Smith, Arkansas, who twice prosecuted Henry Starr for murder of deputy United States marshal.

Booth   Coal Hill,
Arkans

William Tuttle "Bill" Cook, leader of notorious "Cook gang" in Indian Territory; friend of Starr's while in Fort Smith jail.

Robertson, CHEROKEE BILL, MUSKOGEE, Ind. Ter

Photographs on this and facing page from the author's collection.

Crawford Goldsby, alias "Cherokee Bill," whom Starr dramatically disarmed during an attempted jail break at Fort Smith, Arkansas.

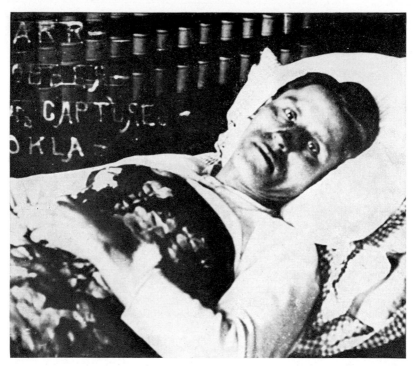

Photograph courtesy of Oklahoma Historical Society.

Starr in a doctor's office at Stroud, Oklahoma, shortly after he was wounded and captured in daring robbery of two banks.

Gang of Noted Outlaws Raided Two Banks at Stroud

Banks Were Robbed Simultaneously Shortly After Nine O'clock Last Saturday Morning—Total of $5,922.00 Secured—$1,000 Found on Captured Bandit—Also Diamond Stud Taken from Patrick.

TWO OUTLAWS WERE SHOT AND CAPTURED

Paul Curry, Nineteen Year Old Stroud Boy, Shoots Henry Star and Floyd Estes—Posses from Three Counties Join in Chase of Balance of Gang Without Success—Star and Estes Now in Jail at Chandler.

STARR'S GUN.

PAUL CURRY
THE BOY WHO CAPTURED
STARR AND ESTES.

Photograph from author's collection.

Paul Curry, who wounded and captured Starr in the double bank
robbery at Stroud, Okla., March 27, 1915. He holds Starr's rifle.

Bank at Harrison, Arkansas, the scene of Starr's last holdup.

LEFT: W. J. Meyers, former president and a stockholder of People's National Bank, who shot and mortally wounded Starr. Photo, University of Oklahoma Library, Ms. Div.

Kate Barnard, the first Commissioner of Charities and Corrections in Oklahoma. Befriended Starr, and blamed society for his failure to reform. Photo, University of Oklahoma Library, Ms. Div.

A. I saw him about half way from Patchett's to my house, coming towards my house, and he came there and looked in at the door. . . . I can't say that he saw these men, but there was nothing to hinder him from seeing them. He kept looking on the ground like he was hunting for horse tracks . . . like he was tracking for somebody. He then turned and rode off in a southerly direction.

Q. They had made a search for him and didn't find him?

A. Yes, sir. They came back that night, Dickey and Wilson did, and stayed there the balance of the night.

Q. Go ahead and in your own way tell what occurred from that time on until the killing took place.

A. . . . These men were there, they were strangers to me, and the next morning I went on about my work and they fixed to go, and I told them I thought in all reason Henry would be along in a little while—he was in a habit of coming by. . . . Whether that induced the gentlemen or not I don't know, but they did stay. They fixed their guns up, and went down to the barn and set in the loft, and I was about the door when I saw Henry Starr right here [indicating on a plat of the grounds showing location of houses, barn, etc.] and I hollered and told them, and they come down out of the loft, and come out here and got in the smoke house right here, thinking he would stop. I told them the smoke house would be better protection for them, and it might save the little children, or something to that effect, because I was afraid of my children getting killed. And so they went into the smoke house right away. Starr failed to come down this way; he went right around here. Then Wilson come down to the stable for a horse to intersect Starr here. He come down there, and about that time this man Miller had come across the field, I suppose, and was standing there somewhere, and Wilson ordered Miller to saddle his horse as quick as he could. He hollered to me to know where that horse was. I had come in a few minutes before on my horse, driving up the cows, and I told him it was in the stable. He wanted to know if it was still saddled, and I said it was, and he said to get it out, he wanted him. I went in the barn and led the horse out for him, and he got on him and rode off, and by that time we went to work on the second horse, saddling it for Dickey. He proved to be a mean horse, sullen, and would pull back; and this man Dickey come running down there and met us pulling and trying to get the horse to come along. Dickey got on him, and about the time he got in the saddle the horse took a spell and run back and fell down and pretty near rolled over. Dickey got up and wanted me to get another horse, and I told him there was no other there any better; that he had better try him again; so he mounted him again; he put the spurs to him, and the horse went a little piece, turned and run back again, and fell down the second time, and got up and sort of plunged like a wild horse will. Dickey got on again, and the horse started and went off in the direction of Floyd and Starr, in a lope.

Q. Floyd Wilson had gone on?

A. Yes, sir; by that time Floyd had checked up, had stopped.

Q. Was Starr in sight at that time?

A. Yes, sir; Starr was still in sight; Starr had stopped.

Q. Go ahead and tell everything you saw.

A. Starr was standing there with a Winchester in his

hand, his arm through his horse's bridle rein, holding his Winchester out in this style [indicating]. Wilson was just in the act of dismounting, and they parleyed, acted like they were talking to each other. . . . I could hear them talking, but I could not tell what they were saying plainly. In just a second Henry started to drop his horse's rein like he was going to lead off, and Wilson got up, I should think, in 8 to 10 steps of him, and it was only a second then until Wilson shot.

Q. Tell what you saw in reference to the shooting.

A. Wilson shot first, and the smoke from his gun ranged up in that direction . . . looked like it would not go anywhere near Henry at all, and about the same instant Henry shot, and the smoke ranged down like it was going into the ground, and Wilson fell, and it looked like as quick as a man could possibly rise to his feet he rose and shot again, and Henry shot another time, and Wilson fell the second time, and I never did see him rise any more. I saw him roll over several times and shoot, and Henry would shoot every time. There was sort of a pause in the shooting, like they were going to quit, and I saw Wilson roll over towards him and shoot again, and Henry just turned his gun that way, and broke and run in like he was going to hit Wilson on the head, and instead of hitting him he threw his gun right down on him apparently, the best I could tell, pointed right at him and shot.

Q. Could you tell what part of the body, in your judgment, that shot entered?

A. It was my judgment it hit him right exactly in the breast, but of course I wasn't close enough to see. I was between three and four hundred yards away. . . .

Q. Did Wilson do anything more?

A. No, sir; I never saw him do anything more. Henry Starr made a break and run for my horse. My horse got away from Wilson, and he run for the horse.

Q. Did Starr leave then?

A. Yes, sir. . . .

Q. Did Starr do this firing with a gun [rifle] or pistol?

A. I think all of it at Wilson with his gun [rifle].

Q. Did you see Starr after that?

A. Yes, sir; about two weeks after that he came back to my house and called me out, and told me that he would tell me where my horse was, and I told him all right, and he up and told me.

Q. Did he tell you anything about the shooting?

A. No, sir; never said a word about it. He told me, "I hated like hell to have to ride your horse off, but I couldn't do any better; I was afraid that whole damned country was alive with marshals." He says, "I took you and Miller all to be marshals, and after this I don't want you to·let another damned marshal get on your horse as long as you live; your horse is what fooled me; I thought it was some of your boys coming out there." I knew who he had reference to, those boys that were working for me. He said, "That is what fooled me."

Q. Did he say whether or not he would have let him [Wilson] get that close?

A. No, sir; he didn't say anything about that at all. He said, "I don't want you to let any damned marshal ride your horse again. . . ."

Q. Did you ever get your horse?

A. I got him three days ago.

Q. Did he refuse to deliver him up . . .?

A. Henry never refused to give him up, but the parties that held the horse refused to give him up. They said Henry left him there. I sent a written order out there in the Osage, and they wouldn't let us have it.

Q. How is it you got him recently and could not get him before?

A. Henry's mother got it. . . . It was a favorite horse of mine, and made my whole neighborhood feel bad on that account.

Q. Had Henry ever said anything before [the killing] to you as to whether or not he would ever be arrested by marshals?

A. No, sir.

Q. Did he ever discuss the matter at all?

A. I can't say he ever did. I have sort of jokingly talked to him, hinted to him that he was scouting, but he never said anything.

Q. Did Starr ever say who it was he had killed, call a name?

A. No, sir. . . .

Q. Was he acquainted with Wilson?

A. I never heard him say anything about him at all. . . .

Q. Do you know whether Starr was acquainted with Mr. Dickey or not?

A. No, sir.

Q. Wilson had been in that country as a marshal before, had he not?

A. Not that I know anything about.

Q. Had you seen the warrant that Mr. Dickey had?

A. I didn't see no warrant at all.

Q. How often was he there at your house to see this woman?

A. He never come there to see this woman here, but another woman that used to come there.

Q. What was the name of the other woman?
A. Mary Zane.
Q. Was that the one who was with him in Colorado?
A. No, sir.
Q. Do you know whether Starr ever talked with Mr. Patchett or not?
A. Yes, sir; he could not have helped talked with him; he stayed in his house two days and two nights after the killing, upstairs there right in the house. I was there and didn't know he was in the house. He was laying upstairs with a Winchester; I didn't know it until afterwards.
Q. That is on your place?
A. Yes, sir.
Q. Does this man still live there on your place?
A. Yes, sir.
Q. Has he married since that?
A. Yes, sir; married the girl that was cooking for me— Mary Black.
Q. She was there at your house at the time [of the killing]?
A. Yes, sir; standing there on this south porch, her and the children, watching this transaction that took place out here.

MARY PATCHETT:

Q. What was your name before you married?
A. Mary Black.
Q. How long have you been married?
A. Since the 9th day of February.
Q. Where did you live before you were married?

88

A. At Arthur Dodge's.

Q. How long had you lived there?

A. Five months and seven days.

Q. Where did you live before you lived there?

A. Kansas.

Q. Were you acquainted with Henry Starr?

A. I wasn't personally acquainted with him. . . . I had seen him lots of times.

Q. You had seen him at Mr. Dodge's house, had you not?

A. He came there several times.

Q. Did he come there to visit you?

A. No, sir; he didn't come to visit me. . . . There was a lady that came there once in a while.

Q. What was her name?

A. Mary Zane.

Q. She was a friend of Henry's, was she?

A. They would get together—

Q. He was paying some attention to her, was he?

A. Yes, sir.

Q. Was that all during last fall?

A. She never went to Mr. Dodge's until after I did —the last of August; she was the first Indian lady I got acquainted with, and she would come there.

Q. And from that time on until the time of the killing of Wilson was Starr there about once a week to see this Mary Zane?

A. Oh, no; it was about two weeks, or three weeks, I guess before he killed this marshal that he was there.

Q. At least once a week?

A. Yes, sir; he met her there sometimes, and sometimes he didn't.

Q. Did you know Mr. Floyd Wilson?

A. I wasn't acquainted with him. The first I saw him was when they came there.

Q. Mr. Dickey and he?

A. Yes, sir.

Q. Do you remember when that was?

A. They came on Sunday night before the killing. . . . They came in the night sometime. I was asleep, and they woke me up talking, and they went out and came in about daylight, as far as I can remember, and they were there for breakfast Monday.

Q. On that Sunday had you seen Starr?

A. He was there Sunday evening.

Q. How long before they were there?

A. About an hour by sun. They came in that night.

Q. Did you see him have any conversation with anybody that evening, Sunday?

A. He came in the room there and set and talked to the children and me for a few minutes.

Q. Did he then say anything about the marshals being after him?

A. No, sir; he never said anything at all about the marshals—that is, those marshals—just kind of laughed and said he guessed they were kind of tracing him up, or something.

Q. What for?

A. I don't know, unless for jumping bond . . . he didn't say for anything; he said they were after him.

Q. He knew the marshals were hunting for him?

A. I guess so.

Q. What did he say about giving up to them?

A. He never said anything about it. He was just asking about his girl, wanted to know if I had seen his girl, his other girl, the one I suppose he married afterwards.

Q. On that Sunday afternoon however he did not say anything about the marshals being after him . . . about killing them if they should attempt to arrest him?

A. No, sir. He came there and wanted to know if Miss Zane had been there, and I told him no, and he said he would like to see her, and he left a note there for her.

Q. Did she get the note afterwards?

A. Yes, sir; I sent it to her in a letter. She had left that morning for Seneca.

Q. Do you know what was in the note?

A. It was just that he would like to see her, and such as that.

Q. Appoint a time for meeting?

A. No, sir.

Q. That was Sunday?

A. Yes, sir.

Q. When did you next see Starr?

A. I saw him at a dance at Morrison's.

Q. Didn't you see him Monday evening when he passed by Mr. Dodge's house?

A. No . . . because I was sitting in the room.

Q. On Tuesday, the day of the shooting, did you see him?

A. I could not say it was Starr.

Q. The man that Wilson had the shooting with?

A. They said it was Starr. Yes, sir.

Q. You saw that man?

A. Yes, sir.

Q. Tell us what you saw of the shooting.

A. Well . . . I came out to throw out some water,

and I seen him out there, and when I seen him ride off pretty brisk I thought the marshals were after him and so I stayed on the porch, and I saw Mr. Wilson ride, and I heard Mr. Dickey here holler, "Wait, Floyd," and he still went, and never paid any attention to Mr. Dickey. And Mr. Dickey's horse was backing and falling down with him, and about that time I looked around and saw Floyd shoot, and then quite a little pause until the other one shot, and I could not tell any further.

Q. Did Wilson fall at the time the other man shot?

A. Yes, sir.

Q. The first time?

A. Yes, sir.

Q. How did Wilson shoot?

A. He shot towards Henry, the one they said was Henry, shot towards him; the way the smoke went it looked like it was towards him. My eyes are not as stout as they ought to be. I could not see anything as plain as the rest, and I was excited, too.

Q. Do you know whether they talked awhile before the shooting commenced?

A. I could not tell, only I heard Wilson say, "Hold up; I have got a warrant for you!" and the other one said, "You hold up." That is all I heard.

Q. Wilson said to the man, "Hold up, I have got a warrant for you"?

A. Yes, sir.

Q. The other man said, "You hold up"?

A. Yes, sir.

Q. That was before any shooting took place?

A. Yes, sir.

Q. The shooting occurred right afterwards?

A. Yes, sir. Just as he rode up he hollered, "Hold up," and commenced to shoot, and after the second shot I couldn't see any more, because there was constant smoke, and I could not tell anything about it . . . the excitement and keeping the children pacified—the little boy was not very well—and then I was watching Mr. Dickey, too. I had to kind of keep my eyes going both ways.

Q. Do you know how many shots were fired by Wilson?

A. I couldn't say; just one is all I could see.

Q. Did you see the man who was firing at Wilson fire the last shot that was fired by him at Wilson?

A. After Wilson shot first at him I saw him fire, and that is all I seen . . . because it was constant smoke, you know. Mr. Patchett made the remark that he had killed Wilson, and I asked him if they would bring him to the house, and he said, "Yes," and I ran in and put the teakettle on, and thought if they hadn't killed him they would bring him there, and I went to fix for it, and I fixed Mr. Patchett's cot and got some rags out to wash him, and I put on the teakettle to have warm water to wash him.

Q. Did you see Starr go away?

A. No, sir; I didn't see anything further; that is all I saw.

Q. Have you seen Starr since then?

A. I saw him once. . . . He came to our house about six months afterwards; wanted me to cook his dinner, and my man said he wouldn't let me cook for him. He said he didn't want him there at all.

Q. What did he talk about while he was there?

A. I think he just walked backward and forward,

talked about Mary Zane, when I had seen her, and his other girl, and I said I saw his other girl once, and he said, "Which do you like the best?" and I said, "I like the Delaware better than the white girl."

Q. Was Mr. Patchett there?

A. He came to the house.

Q. What did he say?

A. He told Henry, "I can't uphold you in your devilment."

Q. What did Henry say?

A. He said it was all right.

Q. Did he go off then?

A. Yes, sir. He got on his horse and rode off.

Q. Did he in your hearing at that time say anything about the killing of Wilson?

A. No, sir; he never said anything about that at all.

Q. You knew at that time that he was on the scout, and that marshals were after him?

A. Yes, sir; I knew at that time they were.

Q. Did he tell you where he was going when he left?

A. No, sir.

Q. Didn't tell you where he had been?

A. No, sir; I could not say anything further.

JOHN PATCHETT:

Q. You are the husband of Mary Patchett?

A. Yes, sir.

Q. On whose place [do you live]?

A. Arthur Dodge's.

Q. How long have you lived in that country?

A. Three years last March.

Q. How long have you known Henry Starr?

A. Along about two years and a half.

Q. How far did he live from where you live?

A. About a mile and a half or two miles.

Q. Did you see much of him?

A. He has been at my house a good deal . . . in the last year or two.

Q. Where were you at the time of the shooting between him and Wilson?

A. I was plowing about a quarter west of him.

Q. Did you see the shooting?

A. I saw it at that distance.

Q. Tell what you saw.

A. I saw a man coming across there, and I saw Wilson come out . . . and he rode up there and came up to where this man supposed to be Starr—I can't say that was Starr, for I wasn't close enough to tell who it was; but anyway he rode out to that man, and they both came to a halt, and they stopped there and parleyed. . . . I don't know how long, maybe 2 or 3 minutes, and then one of them started to lead his horse off, Starr did, and Wilson . . . rides on down to Starr, right close to him, about 10 or 15 steps, I judge, and Wilson just dismounted . . . and shot at Henry Starr, and after a little hesitation Henry shot and I saw Wilson rise and shoot again, and Henry shot and Wilson fell, and from that the shooting between both of them I could not tell anything about it.

Q. Did you see the last shot fired by Starr?

A. Yes, sir.

Q. While Wilson was down on the ground?

A. Yes, sir.

Q. Did you see him run up to Wilson and fire a shot right into his breast?

A. No, sir; I didn't see him run right up to Wilson; when they were both firing Henry kept crowding on him all the time, and when he fired the last shot he was right close to him.

Q. Starr was crowding on Wilson?

A. Yes, sir.

Q. What did they say to each other?

A. I could not understand what they said. . . .

Q. What became of Starr's horse?

A. Starr's horse came up to my house.

Q. What became of the horse Wilson was riding?

A. Starr rode him off.

Q. Had you seen Starr the day before that?

A. I had not.

Q. Had you seen him on Sunday or Monday before?

A. I wasn't home.

Q. How long after that was it until you saw him?

A. About three weeks. He came to my house. . . .

Q. What for?

A. Just like he always did; happened in to get something to eat and go on.

Q. Did he stay all night there?

A. Yes, sir.

Q. What did he say to you then?

A. He had nothing to say; he wouldn't talk about it.

Q. The killing?

A. No, sir; not a word.

Q. Didn't he tell you that Wilson, before he shot him the last time, was lying on his back begging like a dog for him not to shoot him any more, and he shot him notwithstanding?

A. He didn't tell me that.

Q. Didn't Starr tell you something like that?

A. He did not.

Q. How long did he stay at your house?

A. One day and one night, I think. . . .

Q. In all this time he was at your house did he not stay upstairs in the loft?

A. Yes, sir; he was up in the loft.

Q. Had his Winchester right there, did he not?

A. Yes, sir.

Q. Why did he put himself up there?

A. Dogged if I know . . . he went up there and stayed a while and came down.

Q. How long did he stay upstairs?

A. I don't know; I was not in when he came; when I came he was upstairs.

Q. There was no one living at that house except you?

A. Miller was working with me and was staying there.

Q. You were all batching there?

A. Yes, sir.

Q. Did Starr sleep in a bed by himself or with somebody else?

A. He just slept in the bed with the rest of us.

Q. What did he state about being on the scout, or the officers being after him?

A. He never said anything. . . .

Q. Did he ever ask you whether or not you saw the shooting?

A. No, sir; he never did.

Q. Do you know anything about his connection with robberies in any way? Did he ever tell you anything about that?

A. No, sir; he never was at my house but twice since that killing.

Q. Can you tell us to whom he made that statement about shooting Wilson while he was begging like a dog?

A. I cannot.

Q. You do not know?

A. No, sir.

Q. Is Miller here?

A. Yes, sir.

Q. What is his first name?

A. Emmett.

EMMETT MILLER:

Q. Do you live on Arthur Dodge's place?

A. I make my home about 8 miles northwest of Lenapah. . . . I have been working on his place from about last October; I left there about the last of June.

Q. Who was it you worked for?

A. Mr. Patchett.

Q. Do you know Henry Starr?

A. Yes, sir; I have known him for about 6 years.

Q. Did you see the shooting between him and Wilson?

A. Yes, sir; I seen the shooting.

Q. Tell us what you saw about it.

A. This man here, Patchett—I left his house about noon and went down to Dodge's, went down on a kind of errand, and I went to the house, and hadn't been there but a few minutes and Arthur wasn't at the house. . . . I went down to the barn, and on my way down there I heard somebody speak; I could not tell where the sound came from, and I went on . . . . I had not more than got to the barn until here come this man Wilson and spoke to me. He said very angrily, "Get out that horse right quick." He was an officer, I thought, and obeyed him, and got the horse out, and by that time he jumped on Arthur's horse that Arthur had already saddled . . . and rides out in the direction of where that man was towards the tank, and they stopped out there, and by that time I got up to the house, and pretty soon this here Mr. Wilson rides up on this man, and they come to a halt there, and this here man Wilson run up on this other man and he fires—gets off his horse and fired. The best of my knowledge there was a few shots, and then there was a pause, and this man commenced firing at him.

Q. What did he say before he shot? What did Wilson say?

A. I could not tell what he said, because he was quite a little ways off . . . a quarter of a mile or over from the house.

Q. Go ahead. . . .

A. That is about all I know; when they got through shooting I went out there where they were, and this man Wilson was dead, and this other man was gone.

Q. Did you see Starr—this other man—fire the last shot? How he fired that shot?

A. Well, sir, he run up, looked like he kept crowding him, you know, and it looked like he threw his hand back that way [indicating], and done that.

Q. Pointed it right down at him?

A. Yes, sir.

Q. What was Wilson doing at that time?

A. I couldn't tell; it looked like he wasn't doing anything.

Q. That fellow ran right up to Wilson and fired the last shot?

A. Yes, sir.

Q. What did Starr do then?

A. He ran out there this way and caught this horse that Wilson was riding and went off.

Q. Did you ever see Starr any more?

A. I saw him once since.

Q. Did you talk with him?

A. Yes, sir.

Q. When he was back at Patchett's?

A. Yes, sir.

Q. What did he tell you about the shooting?

A. He never said anything about the shooting.

Q. Mr. Miller, he told you something that we want to know. He told you that he shot Wilson the last shot while Wilson was begging like a dog for him not to shoot him, or words of that kind. Now, what was it?

A. Let's see—

Q. We want you to tell the truth about it, without reference to Starr or anybody else. You do not want to favor him or the Government, but you want to tell the truth.

A. Yes, sir; I want to tell it as I know it.

Q. That is exactly right; you cannot afford to do anything else. What was it he said?

A. He says—it seems to me there was some talk about it—Starr said if he hadn't commenced shooting at him why he would have quit. You know, after the second pause there he claimed that Wilson went to shooting at him again, and he finished him, and—

Q. What did he say on the other point, on the question of shooting Wilson when Wilson was begging him not to do it? The information has come to us that Starr stated to you that he shot Wilson that last time while

Wilson was begging him not to shoot him; Wilson told him that he had a family at home, a wife and child, and he wanted to see his wife and child, and for God's sake not to shoot him again, and Starr said to him, "You God-damned son-of-a-bitch you ought not to have come after me!" *What did Starr say?*

A. It has been so long, and I was trying to think—

Q. Take your time, and think it up.

A. [After a pause] Starr did say something just like that—

Q. Think it up and state it just as near as you can, Mr. Miller. . . . Did he not say to you that he [Wilson] was begging him [Starr] not to shoot him, that he had a wife and children, and that he told him the damned son-of-a-bitch ought not to have come after him?

A. I remember of his saying something, that he would not have shot at Wilson if he hadn't commenced shooting at him again—

Q. You have stated that. But the conversation that he had with you about shooting the last shot; what did he say about shooting the last shot?

A. I have told you all I know and as far as I know.

Q. Didn't he tell you that Wilson begged him not to shoot him any more?

A. He might have—honestly I don't remember. . . .

Q. You are drinking right now?

A. I have been drinking, but I know everything I am saying.

Q. But your memory is not very good when you are drinking?

A. Yes, sir.

Q. Have you been drinking for the purpose of testifying in this case, getting yourself in a fix?

A. No, sir.

Q. We don't want you to get drunk or get to drinking again when you are down here as a witness.

A. No, sir.

Q. We want you to tell the truth about this thing.

A. Yes, sir.

Q. You get your mind befogged with whiskey, and you cannot remember anything.

A. You are right about that.

Q. Now what did he say about Wilson begging him not to shoot at him?

A. About him saying that he was a man of a family, not to shoot any more? I told you about that pause, you know, and he said Wilson went to firing, shooting right up in his face again, and he finished him.

Q. You are not so drunk but what you can remember?

A. I am telling you as near as I can remember it.

Q. I am sorry you took a drink of whiskey at all.

A. I have not taken enough to show it.

Q. There is no reason on earth why you cannot tell what Henry Starr said to you?

A. I am willing to tell anything I know.

Q. Tell what he said to you then about that matter. . . . What did he say about calling Wilson a damned son-of-a-bitch, that he ought not to have come after him?

A. He may have told me that, but honestly I could not swear that he told me that.

Q. If you would get sober you would remember it?

A. It might refresh my memory, but I don't remember anything of the kind.

Q. Don't you ever get drunk when you come down here again. You are too drunk to testify in this case right now. You know every part of that conversation, and you have just got enough liquor in you to forget it.

A. I am not trying to forget anything at all.

Q. Then you are trying to favor that damned set of outlaws up there; that is what you are trying to do?

A. I told you that when I first went there I went on an errand; I went down to the barn, and hadn't been there just a few minutes until here comes Mr. Wilson, and Mr. Wilson told me to get that horse—

Q. It is unnecessary to go over all that again. What we want is that conversation that this man Starr had with you when he came back there and stopped at Patchett's house.

A. I do not remember any conversation that he had with me.

Q. With anybody?

A. I have told you all I know.

The defense rested its case entirely on the self-defense theory, maintaining that Wilson fired first, and that Starr did not know that Wilson had a warrant for his arrest. Besides, claimed Starr's attorney, the warrant was illegal. It was signed "Stephen Wheeler, Commissioner U. S. Court, Western District of Arkansas," and attested as under seal, but no seal was affixed. Garland objected to the warrant for the want of a seal, and took exception to its admission; though, in answer to questions by Judge Parker, he admitted that Wheeler was a United States Commissioner for the district at the time the writ was issued and that the signature was genuine.[13]

Defendant's counsel asked the court to give the jury certain instruction concerning self-defense; the court modified it, and counsel excepted to the modifications and the giving of the instruction as modified (the additions and modifications by Judge Parker are italicized):

". . . If the defendant, being placed in a position in which his life is imperilled, slay an officer of whose official character he has no notice, *or had no reasonable ground to know his character,* this is homicide in self-defense, if the killing was apparently necessary to save the defendant's life; nor does it matter that the officer was legally seeking to arrest the defendant, the defendant having no notice [of that fact] *of the facts or no reason to know what the purpose of the party was: Provided the defendant did not by his threatening and violent conduct prevent the officer from making his character and mission known. This is given in connection with the principle I have given you, that if a man stands up and obstructs arrest, prevents arrest, armed with deadly weapons, and using them in a way that is threatening, then the officer has no time, nor is he called upon to make proclamation. The officer can stand on the defensive and overcome the danger and take his man or overcome him by violence, if necessary.*

"If the jury believe from the evidence that the defendant was placed in a position at the time of the killing in which his life was imperilled by the deceased, and he slew him without having any notice of his official character, and the killing was apparently necessary to save his own life, then the killing of the deceased was homicide in self-defense; nor does it matter that the deceased was legally seeking to arrest the defendant, if the defendant had no notice of the fact, *or no reasonable grounds to know that he was an officer.*

"It is not necessary to know that it is Floyd Wilson, but an officer. But if the defendant prevented Floyd Wilson from giving notice of his character or mission by threatening or violent conduct, then of course, he would not be required to give notice. He can stand, as upon the other proposition, or the defensive. These propositions are given on the theory that if you believe that no proclamation was made. If a proclamation was made, then the defendant had express notice, he had positive notice, of it."[14]

Quoting the propositions regarding self-defense laid down in *Commonwealth v. Selfridge*,[15] Judge Parker continued:

"First. A man, who in the lawful pursuit of his business, is attacked by another under circumstances which denote an intention to take away his life, or do him some enormous bodily harm, may lawfully kill the assailant, provided he uses all the means in his power, otherwise, to save his own life, or prevent the intended harm, such as retreating as far as he can, or disabling his adversary without killing him, if it be in his power. Secondly. When the attack upon him is so sudden, fierce, and violent that a retreat would not diminish, but increase, his danger, he may instantly kill his adversary, without retreating at all. Thirdly. When from the nature of the attack, there is reasonable ground to believe that there is design to destroy his life, or commit any felony upon his person, the killing of the assailant will be excusable homicide, although it should afterwards appear that no felony was intended."

The judge was stern and severe in his attitude toward persons charged with crime, due in a large measure to his feeling that the Indian country was infested with desperadoes and fugitives from justice and that it was his duty to enforce the law. In his twenty-one years on the bench, 1875 to 1896, he docketed 13,490 cases, exclusive of more than 4,000 petty crimes that got no further than the commissioner's courts. Of this total, 9,454 were convicted by a trial jury or entered pleas of guilty, 344 of whom were tried for offenses punishable by death. Of the 344, 160 were convicted and sentenced to the gallows, and 79 of these hanged. As he himself stated toward the end of his career, "For four lustrums I have been aiding the battle between the law and human rights on one hand, and wicked and unrelenting men of crime on the other. . . . I think it my duty to the public, my duty to the law, my duty to peace and order, my duty to the innocent and unoffending people, my duty to the murdered dead. . . ."

In his charge to the Starr jury, referring to the law above quoted, he said:

"Now what is the first proposition? . . . I say to you it contemplates a state of actual danger, real danger . . . to this defendant, at the time of the killing, springing from the hands of Floyd Wilson, and danger that did not create or bring into existence by a wrongful act of his, because, when we undertake to enter upon the execution of as grave a design as the taking of the life of individuals, we must enter upon it with clean hands and a pure heart. If we have created a condition that leads to a deadly result, the law of self-defense does not apply. . . . And especially does that principle apply to a case when we are doing an act which, from its nature, and the way we are doing it, death could be naturally produced in the conflict that may ensue. . . . I say, then, we must enter upon the execution of this grave act upon our part with clean hands and a pure heart, or, as this law expresses it, we must be in the lawful pursuit of our business. It says that a man who in the lawful pursuit of his business (doing what he had a right to do—in the right at the time) is attacked by another under circumstances which denote an intention to take away his life, or, it may be, to do some enormous bodily harm, may lawfully kill the assailant —when? Provided he use all the means in his power, otherwise, to save his own life, or prevent the intended harm, such as retreating as far as he can, or disabling his adversary without killing him, if it be in his power. Now that is the first proposition of the law of self-defense.

". . . Now this contemplates, as far as this case is concerned, that at the time Floyd Wilson was killed that this defendant was in the right—that he was doing exactly what he had a right to do—and when so situated he was attacked by Wilson in such a way as to indicate a deadly purpose upon his part. . . . He was a fugitive from justice, if he had jumped the bond he had in this court, as they say. If he . . . was up in that country hiding out from his usual place of abode, to avoid arrest, he was then a fugitive from justice; and you have a right to take that condition into consideration. And in passing upon the question as to what was the probable action of these parties at that time—as to what would be the rights of the officer and of this defendant—you have a right to see this transaction in the condition that surrounded it, and as it was characterized by the position

107

of the parties towards it. You have a right to look at that condition, and see if he was expecting officers to pursue him. And if . . . he was then a fugitive from justice, it is a fact that becomes pertinent for you to take into consideration, and the questions whether he had reasonable ground, from what transpired, to know that Floyd Wilson was an officer, and was seeking to arrest him." [16]

Warming up to the circumstances of the case, which apparently aroused his indignation in an uncommon degree, the judge concluded:

"How unjust, how cruel, what a mockery, what a sham, what a bloody crime, it would be, upon the part of this government, to send a man out into that Golgotha to officers, and command them, in the solemn name of the President of the United States, to execute these processes, and say to them: 'Men may defy you; men may arm themselves, and hold you at bay; they may obstruct your process; they may intimidate your execution of it; they may hinder you in making the arrest; they may delay you in doing it by threats of armed violence upon you; and yet I am unable, as chief executive of this government, to assure you that you have any protection whatever!' . . . What was this posse to do? What was he commanded to do? To go into the Indian country, and hunt up Mr. Starr, and say to him that on a certain day 'the judge of the federal court at Fort Smith will want your attendance at a little trial down there, wherein you are charged with horse stealing, and you will be kind enough, sir, to put in your attendance on that day; and the judge sends his compliments to

you, Mr. Starr?' Is that his mission? Is that the message
from this court that is to be handed to Mr. Starr upon
a silver platter, with all the formalities of polite society?
Is that what Floyd Wilson was employed or engaged to
do? No. This court did not have anything to do with
that command. It does not go in the name of this court.
. . . Without these officers, what is the use of this
court? It takes men who are brave to uphold the law
here. I say, because of this, and because there is no protection unless the law is upheld by men of this kind, if
it be true that you are satisfied of the fact, beyond a
reasonable doubt, that Floyd Wilson was a man of this
kind, that he was properly in the execution of the high
duty devolving upon him, and while so properly exe-
cuting it, by the light of these principles of the law I
have given you, his life was taken by this defendant,
your solemn duty would be to say that he is guilty of
the crime of murder. . . . You are to stand by the
nation. You are to say to all the people that no man
can trample upon the law, wickedly, violently, and
ruthlessly. . . . If the law has been violated, it is to
be vindicated." [17]

As a parting shot to the jury, Judge Parker said, "Retire,
gentlemen, and *do your duty.*"

The jury began its deliberations Friday morning, October 20, and on the first vote stood nine for conviction,
three for acquittal. A second ballot, taken in the afternoon,
stood eleven to one, and shortly after, a verdict was made
up. When they returned to the box and the foreman announced that they had found the defendant "guilty as
charged of murder in the first degree," Parker turned to
the manager of the hotel where the jury ate its meals, and

asked: "Have you a good dinner prepared for these men?"

The hotel man nodded.

"Then," the judge continued, "take them over and give it to them. They deserve it!"

On November 4, the prisoner was brought in for sentence. Sutton, in *Hands Up!* [18] claims that Starr, when Parker asked if he had anything to say why the judgment of the court should not be carried out, countered: "Are you going to sentence me to death?" Parker replied that it was his duty to do so under the law, and Starr demanded to know what law he had for it: "In this case there is only one law—the law of self-defense, the law of God and man. It was my duty to kill Floyd Wilson. It was proved here. Under what law are you proceeding then when you sentence me to be hanged?"

The judge glared down at him and broke into one of his usual lengthy tirades, denouncing Starr, when Starr interrupted with:

"Don't you try to stare me down, old Nero. I've looked many a better man than you in the eye. Cut out the rot and save your wind for your next victim. If I am a monster, you are a fiend, for I have put only one man to death, while almost as many have been slaughtered by your jawbone as Samson slew with the jawbone of that other historic ass."

Judge Parker was so dumfounded that he stopped his harangue and pronounced the sentence.

Sutton's story appeared in 1927. It was retold by Boyce House in his column in many Texas newspapers in the early 1930's, in A. W. Neville's "Backward Glances" in the Paris (Texas) *News*, January 3, 1936, and accepted as history by Drago in *Outlaws on Horseback*.[19] It makes exciting reading. Only it didn't happen. Starr makes no mention of the episode in *Thrilling Events,* but states simply: [20] "The judge, with his usual ornate vanity, gave me a twenty-minute lecture, but failed in his object. That fellow never could scare me. He sentenced me to the hemp, but I never batted an eye. I was young and foolish in the head in those days."

The facts appear in the Fort Smith *Weekly Elevator,* of November 10, 1893:

Last Saturday morning Judge Parker passed the sentence of death upon Henry Starr. It being known that the dread sentence was to be pronounced that day the court room was crowded to its fullest capacity. In the audience were several ladies.

After disposing of business remaining over from the preceding day Judge Parker passed upon the motion of Starr's attorney for a new trial, overruling it. He then ordered Starr to stand up, when the following question was asked:

"Henry Starr, you have been convicted by a jury of your country of the crime of murder, having wilfully and with malice aforethought killed Floyd Wilson. Before you are sentenced have you anything to say why the sentence of the law should not now be passed?"

To this Starr responded, in a firm voice, "Nothing at all."

The judge then pronounced the following:

"This sentence is the voice of the law which must be spoken after guilt is legally ascertained. It is this which constitutes the force and power of the criminal law. It is its penalty which must follow conviction that security may be afforded to innocent life.

"I do not believe that you yet have even begun to

appreciate the enormity and wickedness of the act you have committed. You do not realize what you have done. In fact, when we consider the character of the great crimes which have been proven to have been committed by you, your young life becomes a marvel of wickedness. Here you are, scarcely arrived at majority, with a conscience stained with larceny, with highway robbery, and what is worse still, the great crime of having . . . taken a human life—the life of one who was seeking to check you in your wild, mad, reckless career . . . that you might be brought to a sense of your true condition. Would, for the sake of Floyd Wilson, your victim, he had been successful in his efforts to arrest you; yea, for your own sake, it is a pity he did not succeed in bringing you before a court and jury. If this had been so he would at this time be alive for his family and his country, and you would not be standing in this tribunal with a soul stained and blackened with the terrible crime of murder.

"You seem to have voluntarily started on a career of crime. You appear to have intentionally entered upon its dark and gloomy highway. You were first arrested and brought to this court for the larceny of a horse, when under this charge you forfeited your bond and became a refugee from justice. Other charges of larceny were pending against you. You set the law at defiance. You had nothing but hatred and vengeance for its officers. You proclaimed your purpose to resist them; you defied their authority; you were refugeeing to keep from being arrested. When about to be arrested by Floyd Wilson you were in a proper frame of mind to kill rather than be taken. You did so, and when you did you stole the life of a gallant, brave, faithful officer and good citizen, who laid down his life for law, for order, for peace, for protection and security, and gallantly died as much for his country as the brave soldier 'mid the battlefield. He died at the hands of one who manifestly cared neither for property or human life, and whose mission was death to all who sought to bring him to justice.

"By your wicked and bold career of crime you show that you possess a heart void of social duty and a mind fatally bent on mischief.

"These deeds committed by you show you to be the very personification of the man of crime, and in this age of terrible and wicked crimes, when innocent human life is so cheap, and just punishment so rare, you seem in your short career to have even excelled the most wicked. . . .

"No one in my judgment should for a moment doubt the entire justice of the verdict rendered by the jury, and fail to say that, under the law and the evidence, they did exactly right; and the jury should be commended for doing it, because they have properly named a great crime, and correctly designated the author of it.

"It now remains with you whether you will first make an effort to appreciate the true character of the act done by you, and then make an honest, faithful effort to purge your soul of it, for wicked as it is, Divine mercy, coming from the All Merciful, will cleanse it. It is the compassion of the all-merciful God that you now need more than anything else. My advice is for you to seek it honestly and faithfully. First, fully realize your condition. Do not continue to regard yourself as a hero, and your act of murder an act of heroism, but look at it as it is, a deep, bloody, wicked crime. Then of your soul be possessed with sorrow for this terrible deed. Determine to commune with your God, so as to obtain His compassion, His mercy, His forgiveness, that you may stand in His presence with the crime of murder washed from your soul. This is now the highest duty you can possibly owe yourself. I have thus spoken plainly to you that you may fully comprehend your situation and truly realize your duty.

"Listen now to the sentence of the law as pronounced by the court. That sentence is that you, Henry Starr, for the crime of murder, in wilfully and with malice aforethought killing Floyd Wilson, in the Indian country, and within the jurisdiction of this court, of which crime you stand convicted by the verdict of the jury in your case, be deemed, taken and adjudged guilty of murder, and that you therefore for the said crime against the laws of the United States, be hanged by the neck until you are dead, that the marshal of the Western District of Arkansas, by himself or deputy or deputies, do, in peril of what may befall them, at some convenient place in the Western District of Arkansas, cause execution to be done in the premises on Tuesday, February 20 A.D., 1894, between the hours of 9 o'clock in the forenoon and 5 o'clock in the afternoon of the same day; and that you now be taken to the jail from whence you came, there to be closely and securely kept until the day of execution, and from thence on the day of execution as aforesaid, there to be hanged by the neck as aforesaid until you are dead.

"And may God, whose law you have broken, and before whose dread tribunal you must then appear, have mercy on your soul."

114

The prisoner received the sentence unmoved, and at its conclusion he was remanded to jail.

Starr's attorney promptly appealed to the United States Supreme Court. He demanded, and got, a stay of execution, and asked for a new trial on the grounds that:

1st. The court erred in excusing jurors who were opposed to capital punishment.

2nd. Accepting as a juror a man who had read newspaper accounts of the killing and formed an opinion therefrom, although he stated that it was not such that it would take evidence to remove.

3rd. Admitting as evidence the warrant for Starr's arrest which Detective Dickey had at the time Wilson was killed.

4th. Permitting the district attorney to refresh the memory of Arthur Dodge by asking leading questions.

5th. Refusing to give certain instructions asked for by the defendant, and in giving certain instructions.[21]

On the 1st, 2nd, and 4th points, the Supreme Court took no action, and ruled on the 3rd that a warrant without seal, issued by a United States Commissioner having no seal of office, and not required by an act of congress or statute of the state to be under seal, was not void for the omission. It did not, however, agree with Parker's interpretation of the question of self-defense, nor feel that his charge to the jury, expressing indignation at the homicide and urging argumentatively the necessity of vindicating and upholding the law, was "consistent with due regard to the right and duty of the jury to exercise an independent judgment."

Although repeatedly referring to Parker in the highest terms of praise as a judge, Mr. Chief Justice Melville W. Fuller, on May 14, 1894, wrote the opinion of the court in this language:

". . . The question did not arise here in respect of homicide by the officer, but by the person whom he was trying to arrest; and if the defendant had no knowledge, was not informed, and was not chargeable with notice of Wilson's mission or official character, the fact, if there was evidence tending to show it, that defendant prevented the giving of notice had no such relation to defendant's claim of exemption from liability founded on his ignorance, and the appearance of the facts to him as to justify the modification [of the instruction].

"We presume that the learned judge intended to express the view that the existence of a state of facts which might render the homicide excusable was subject to the qualification that wrongful action on defendant's part towards Wilson did not occasion the attack. But we are of opinion that the language used was open to a different construction, and tended fatally to mislead. Whether the right of self-defense is legitimately exercised depends upon the circumstances of the particular transaction; and we take it that the possession of a conscience void of offense towards God and men is not an indispensable prerequisite to justification of action, in the face of imminent and deadly peril. Nor does the intrinsic rightfulness of the occupation or situation of a party, having in itself no bearing upon or connection with an assault, impose a limitation on the right to repel it.

"This Cherokee, when riding across the country, was entitled to protect his life, although he may have forfeited a bail bond, and been seeking to avoid arrest on that account, of which there was some slight evidence incidentally given. . . .

"Assuming that the circumstance that he may have anticipated arrest for the reason suggested tended to show that he knew or believed that such was the mission of Wilson, the [judge's] comments put it beyond question that the defendant was not doing what he had a right to do; and if the jury understood that the scope of what had previously been said embraced the rightfulness of his conduct generally, rather than his conduct in respect of the immediate transaction, they could not but have been materially influenced to his prejudice. . . .

"The motive of the accused in being where he was had nothing to do with the question of his right of self-defense, in itself; and the unlawfulness of his previous conduct formed, in itself, no element in the solution of that question, but was to be considered only in so far as it threw light on his belief that his arrest was sought by the officer.

"We are not insensible to the consideration that the learned judge probably did not intend that his words should bear so sweeping a signification, but they were used more than once, and were not withdrawn, or so qualified that it can be fairly held that they were not substantially prejudicial. . . .

"Whatever special necessity for enforcing the law in all its rigor there may be in a particular quarter of the country, the rules by which, and the manner in which, the administration of justice should be conducted, are the same everywhere; and argumentative matter of this sort should not be thrown into the scales of the judicial officer who holds them." [22]

The Supreme Court issued a mandate on June 7, reversing the judgment of the Circuit Court at Fort Smith and remanding the cause with a direction to grant a new trial.

VIII

Henry Starr and Cherokee Bill

Starr expressed little sentiment other than "This was a
great victory for my attorney and a great rebuke to the
prosecution." [1] That he realized he still was a long way
from being out of the woods is evidenced by his only other
reaction, recorded by a South McAlester newspaperman
who visited him in his cell in May, 1895, nearly a year
after the decision was handed down:

Last Sunday the *Capital* reporter, being personally
acquainted with Mr. Gotcher, assistant jailer, was permitted to spend several hours within the walls of the
Fort Smith prison.

This is the most noted jail in the United States. Excepting the penitentiaries, it contains more prisoners
than any other. In it have been confined some of the
most desperate characters the world has ever known.
More men have been led from its doors to the scaffold

and to penal servitude than from any other jail in the country.

A picturesque scene meets the eye as you pass the steps over the heavy stone wall surrounding it. The large elms, green with the fresh verdure of spring, are scattered well over the grounds, while the well-kept grass would do honor to a brown stone dwelling. To the right as you enter the enclosure are the stables, in front of which stands the heavy iron cage on wheels, which has doubtless prevented many a criminal from obtaining his liberty while being transported from the depot. . . . On the left is that old relic of heathendom, the scaffold. Ah! what an army of men have been hung by the neck till they were dead beneath this rough-hewn structure! What an army of immortal souls have been dumped headlong into eternity from this barbaric institution!

Having filled my pockets with tobacco and cigars, wherewith to obtain the good will of guards and prisoners, I entered the jail. Dinner was just over, the prisoners were preparing their toilet and their cells for religious services. . . .

After interviewing several prisoners he found "leisurely walking up and down the corridors," most of whom "conversed freely" with him, he got Marshall Tucker, a white man who had been sentenced to hang, to introduce him to Starr:

Tucker said: "Henry, this is a reporter for the *Capital*. He is talking around with some of the boys and I don't believe he will try to do us any harm."

Starr is a straight, finely built fellow, with an unmistakable reckless dash of appearance. He wore a black sateen shirt and light, well-fitting pants, without coat or vest. His straight black hair, more than anything else, marks him as an Indian.

I told him I had thought of writing up his life and would like sometime for him to write me out a full history of himself. He says, "I may do it later, I don't know anything now." Tucker spoke up and said, jokingly, "Tell him, Henry, about some of the close places you have been in." Starr replied with an unconcerned laugh, "This is the only close place I have ever been in."

A girl came through selling ice cream and strawberries about that time. Starr took a dish of cream and the girl went on. . . .

"Now, while you eat your cream and smoke," I said, offering him a cigar, "tell me something to startle the natives." He refused the cigar saying he did not smoke.

"They want to hear from you out in the Territory," I continued, "tell me something that will make their hair stand up and their eyes bug out."

"Oh," he said carelessly, "I don't care about notoriety. If you want to ask any reasonable questions, I'll try to answer them."

I had just settled myself to ask him about every train and bank robbery that had ever been charged to him when a guard came by and said I would have to move on. He said if I wanted to take up my board in the jail he would try and accommodate me. I bade my friend Henry Starr adieu. I promised to send him a *Capital* and he promised to write an article for it, and I vamoosed.

The lower floors of the jail were filled with murderers, there being 59 then under sentence of death, awaiting a hearing by the Supreme Court.[2] Among them were Dennis

121

Davis, a half-witted but dangerous Negro who had killed his best friend; Buz Luckey, charged with a train robbery at Blackstone Switch in November, 1894, and the slaying of Deputy Marshal Newton LaForce; George and John Pearce, convicted of killing their traveling companion in the Cherokee Nation for a paltry few dollars and his wagon and mules; John and Ed Shelley, all-around bad-men, and Ed's wife Lou, the woman on the outside who, as their confederate and agent, had aided their desperate escape from an Oklahoma jail; and the most deadly and obstreperous killer the Indian Territory had yet produced —Cherokee Bill.

His real name was Crawford Goldsby. He was born at Fort Concho, Texas, February 8, 1876. His father, George Goldsby, a soldier in the Tenth Cavalry once stationed at Fort Gibson, was of Mexican extraction, mixed with white and Sioux; his mother, Ellen Beck, was one-fourth Chero-kee, half Negro, and one-fourth white. When Bill was seven, his parents separated. His mother returned to Fort Gibson, where he was raised by an old colored woman named Amanda Foster. Henry Starr had known Bill in 1888 when, at the age of twelve, he killed his brother-in-law in an argument over some hogs. At eighteen he was a burly, brawling youth who could not be curbed. He was alleged to have murdered Agent Richards in a depot rob-bery at Nowata, killed a young man named Henderson and wounded a brakeman on a freight train at Fort Gib-son, and was on the scout for firing three bullets into the body of Jake Lewis, a youth with whom he had quarreled at a dance, when he joined the Cook gang in 1894.

This versatile band of looters and plunderers—consist-ing of such unenviable lights as Lon Gordon, Henry Munson, Sam McWilliams, alias Verdigris Kid, George

Sanders, Jess Snyder, William Farris, Thurman "Skeeter" Baldwin, Elmer "Chicken" Lucas, Curtis Dayson, and Jim French, last of the old Belle Starr gang of horse thieves and whiskey peddlers—had sprung up under the leadership of William Tuttle Cook, in the Cherokee Nation, June 16, exactly ten days after Henry Starr robbed the Bentonville bank and started to California with his childhood sweetheart.

Cook was another product of Fort Gibson. His father, James Cook, had been stationed there with the Union army during the Civil War. His mother was a quarter-blood Cherokee. A docile-appearing youth of twenty, of stout, athletic build, with full, boyish face, ruddy complexion, light brown hair, a small mustache and blue eyes, he looked like anything except a badman. But within six months he became known the length and breadth of the United States as "Bill Cook, The Famous Outlaw."

During the period his gang functioned—while Starr languished in the Fort Smith jail and devoured the stories of their exploits that filled the border press—Cook raided all that country lying between Fort Gibson and Wagoner and Muskogee. It became unsafe for railroads in the area to carry valuable express matter or passengers in the night-time; they went through only in daylight, and then under heavy guard. He raided nearly every town along their tracks to the Kansas line. He became so ravenous and elusive that Washington was on the verge of sending out Regular Army detachments to assist the marshals and Indian police in rounding up his outfit; and the government, railroads, and express companies placed on his head rewards totaling over $7,000.

He had found Cherokee Bill a fit companion until November 9, 1894, when the gang held up the Shufeldt store and post office at Lenapah, which Starr had robbed two years before. Standing in the store, looking out the door, Cherokee Bill observed a prominent citizen, Ernest Melton, watching him from the window of a restaurant across the street. Never keen about curious witnesses, Cherokee whipped up his Winchester and fired. The ball shattered the glass. It struck Melton just below the left eye and came out the back of his head.

Melton's murder marked the beginning of the end of the Cook outlaws. The search for them became so fierce they were forced to separate. Elmer Lucas was captured in a bank robbery at Chandler, Oklahoma Territory. Gordon and Munson were shot and killed and Curtis Dayson captured as they fled from a farmhouse in the Creek Nation near Sapulpa; Baldwin, Snyder, and Farris were captured by Texas Rangers in Clay County near Wichita Falls; McWilliams, the Verdigris Kid, was slain by Indian deputy sheriffs at Braggs, a small town on the railroad nine miles east of Fort Gibson; and French was killed by a night watchman while burglarizing a store at Catoosa. Cook himself was finally captured January 11, 1895, on an isolated cattle ranch southeast of Fort Sumner, New Mexico, where Pat Garrett had killed another famous outlaw, Billy the Kid. Sheriff C. C. Perry, of Chaves County, and two deputies, surprised him in a sod house and took him without a fight. On January 17, he was arraigned before Judge Parker. He was indicted on twelve counts of armed robbery, convicted on ten, and sentenced to forty-five years in the penitentiary at Albany. Lucas, Dayson, Baldwin, Snyder, and Farris drew ten- to thirty-year terms in prison at Detroit.

Cherokee Bill remained at large in the Indian Territory. Though rewards for him aggregated $1,300, few men were anxious to engage him in combat. In December, 1894, a posse surprised him riding to the home of his sister near Nowata. He escaped in a running gun battle, leaving his hat as a trophy and the officers without a doubt that he would fight to the last.

Deputy Marshals W. C. Smith and George Lawson finally worked the scheme that resulted in his capture.

Isaac Rogers, a Cherokee, had done considerable service as a deputy for Marshal Crump. He had a cousin named Maggie Glass with whom Bill was infatuated. Smith got Rogers to invite the girl to his house for a chicken supper and also extend an invitation to Cherokee Bill. The pair arrived the evening of January 29, and were cordially received. Maggie suspected treachery and warned Bill, but the outlaw refused to leave.

He kept an eye on Rogers, but Rogers was careful not to tip his hand. While his wife and Maggie prepared the meal, he joked with the outlaw and otherwise played the role of the perfect host. After supper, Clint Scales, a friend of Rogers also in on the plan, dropped in for a visit.

Cards were proposed, and Bill played casino and talked with the men until past midnight, declining to retire. Toward morning he finally lay down beside Rogers. But he did not sleep, and kept his Winchester at his side. After breakfast, as all were seated before the open fireplace, Bill began to talk of leaving. It looked as if their game would surely escape, when suddenly Bill decided to smoke. He rested his Winchester across his lap, took the makings from his pocket and rolled a cigarette. He didn't have a match, so he leaned toward the fireplace to light it. His eyes were off his host only an instant. But in that instant, Rogers acted.

As Rogers told it later, "I grabbed up a fire stick lying

on the floor near me and struck him across the back of the head. I must have hit him hard enough to kill an ordinary man, but it only knocked him down. Scales and I then jumped on him but he let one yell and got to his feet.

"My wife grabbed Bill's Winchester, and we three tussled on the floor a full twenty minutes. I thought once I would have to kill him, but finally got the handcuffs on him. He then pleaded and begged me to kill him or release him. He promised me money and horses, all I wanted. Then he cursed. We put him in a wagon and Scales rode with him and I rode horseback and started to where Deputies Smith and Lawson were waiting at Nowata. On the way Cherokee broke his handcuffs and grabbed at Scales' gun and Scales had to fall out of the wagon to keep from losing his Winchester, while I kept Cherokee covered with my shotgun." [3]

Smith and Lawson took charge of the prisoner at Nowata and landed him in the Fort Smith jail. He was tried for the murder of Melton. Arguments in his case began at noon February 26, and ended at 10 o'clock that night. It took Judge Parker just fifteen minutes to charge the jury, and the jury only twenty minutes to bring in a verdict of guilty.

Cherokee Bill smiled. But his mother and sister, who had been with him in the courtroom throughout the trial, wept loudly. "Shut up," he told them. "What's the matter with you? I ain't dead yet!" And the next afternoon, over at the jail, he was engaged in a game of poker with Buz Luckey, Cook, Starr, John and George Pearce, and John and Ed Shelley as if nothing had happened.

On April 13, he was again brought before Judge Parker.

Asked if he had anything to say why judgment should not be passed at that time, he replied, boldly and defiantly, "No, sir." Parker sentenced him to be hanged on June 25.

His attorneys appealed to the Supreme Court. Bill showed no emotion whatever. The only sign that he regarded the matter seriously was the absence of his smile.

Back in jail, he manifested a spirit of unrest. His unruly conduct affected the other prisoners. Many of them predicted "something terrible" would occur, and Bill Cook, when he left for Albany prison on May 2, told a reporter: "No bars can hold Cherokee."

The court was anxious to be rid of the boy killer. But when June 25 arrived, his appeal was still in the hands of the Supreme Court, and Judge Parker issued a stay of execution.

J. D. Berry, former deputy sheriff of Franklin County, Arkansas, was head jailer and as competent as any who served during Parker's tenure. There were more than 200 prisoners in the jail in the spring of 1895, and hardly a day passed that there was not some scheme afoot for a single escape or a wholesale delivery. Berry read the mood of the prisoners, sensed trouble brewing. On July 10, he ordered a search of the entire prison. In Cherokee Bill's cell the guards found nine .45 cartridges, and in the bathroom on Murderers' Row (as the lower floor was called) they found a .45 revolver, fully loaded, hidden in a bucket of lime.

Sherman Vann, a Negro trusty serving ninety days for larceny, was suspected. Vann admitted carrying in the lime, but if the weapon and ammunition were hidden there, he never knew it. Cherokee's cohorts denied that they knew where the weapon came from. Henry Starr was one of the first questioned by Berry, but most of the guards doubted he had anything to do with it.[4]

During the week following it was again whispered that Cherokee Bill would yet kill somebody in the jail. Although Berry and his guards remained alert, they foolishly allowed him the freedom of the Row during the day, the same as the other prisoners. They also failed to discover a second revolver that had been smuggled in his cell. Cherokee Bill had hidden it in the wall behind a loose stone. The inside half of the stone had been broken off and the whitewashed end replaced.

At 7 o'clock the evening of July 26, Turnkey Campbell Eoff (pronounced Ofe) and Guard Lawrence Keating entered Murderers' Row. The day guards at the prison usually were relieved by the night guards at 6 o'clock, and 6:15 was the time for locking the cells on each of the three floors. Owing to the long days and hot weather, the prisoners were allowed to remain in the corridors until 7 o'clock. It was the responsibility of Eoff and Keating, who guarded the lower tier of cells in the daytime, to "ring" the prisoners in for the night. Night Guards Will Lawson, Bras Parker, and William McConnell had just come on duty and were sitting on the ground outside, ten feet from the corridor entrance and the stairway to the jailer's office. Captain Berry had been gone about ten minutes.

Two rows of cells ran north and south on each side of the inner corridor, or "bullpen." The whole inner part of the jail was built of chilled steel, the doors of cross-barred steel, and the corridor walls of steel bars crossed as open grates. Every prisoner had his own cell, and when the gong sounded, each was to go to his proper cell and close his door behind him. Then a guard at the entrance threw a lever, dropping a long bar, or "brake," intended to fasten the closed cell doors on either side at the top. It was Eoff's job, after the lever was pulled, to enter the corridor and lock each door separately. It was a comparatively safe procedure. But there was always the chance that prisoners might hide at the rear of the cage, or otherwise deceive the unarmed turnkey. To lessen the danger, Keating, wearing his six-shooter, walked along outside the cage to make sure each man was in his cell and had closed his door in order that the "brake" should work properly.

The "brake" on either row could be opened, however, by a broomstick or similar instrument in the hands of a prisoner at the north end of the tier, and in compliance with a concerted movement to capture the jail, it was thrown open on the west tier, where Cherokee Bill and his associates were confined, while Eoff and Keating were attending the cells on the east side. As the turnkey passed around the south end and started locking the doors of the west row, Keating kept pace outside the corridor. Cherokee Bill, his door, like the others, free to be pushed open, calmly waited with revolver ready.

Davis was in the cell next to Cherokee Bill. The keyhole in the lock on his door had been stuffed with paper. When Eoff inserted the key it lodged in the lock, and he called to Keating, "Hold up. There is something wrong here."

Eoff leaned forward to examine the lock, and Keating, his attention for a moment centered on the trouble, stepped closer to the bars. At that instant Cherokee Bill sprang from his cell and pointed his revolver through the grate at the guard.

"Throw up your hands and give me that pistol damned quick!" he commanded.

Had the officer complied, Cherokee would have held him and Eoff in subjection while he unlocked the door leading out of the corridor, released all the other prisoners, and led a wholesale break for liberty. Keating reached for his six-shooter instead, and Cherokee shot him through the stomach. Keating staggered backward and stumbled toward the front of the jail to give the alarm. Cherokee fired a second shot at him, and he fell at the foot of the stairway.

When Cherokee Bill sprang from his cell, Eoff tried to jerk the key from the lock. Failing to dislodge it, he left it hanging in the door and fled up the corridor. Thinking he had the key, Cherokee followed Eoff, firing four shots at him. George Pearce, one of the ring-leaders in the plot, jumped from his cell and joined the chase, brandishing a broken table leg for a club. Eoff took refuge in the deep doorway of the front cage. But for the prompt appearance of Will Lawson, Bras Parker, and McConnell at the jail door, he would undoubtedly have lost his life. The guards opened fire and drove Cherokee Bill and Pearce back to the south end of the corridor.

Lawson saw Keating at the foot of the stairs, leaned over and picked up his six-shooter. Recognizing the officer, Keating said, "Kill the dog, Will, he has killed me," and died.

Deputy Marshal Heck Bruner and Captain Berry, hearing the firing, arrived at the jail and joined in the shooting. They accomplished nothing except to hold the blood-thirsty young killer back. Soon Cherokee made a break to his cell. With the door partially opened, he could cover the corridor with little danger to himself. The officers' bullets struck his cell door and ricocheted through the jail without effect.

The excitement rapidly spread to the city. In an incredibly short time, police and scores of citizens armed themselves with Winchesters, shotguns, and revolvers and hastened to help the guards. Marshal Crump arrived from his home in the suburbs and took personal charge of the situation.

Then began a sniping match. Cherokee Bill, having reloaded his revolver, fired at random from his cell, never putting out his head. Every time he fired, he gobbled. It was an uncanny, though familiar, sound in the Territory, half between the bark of a coyote and the throaty cry of a turkey cock. When an Indian "gobbled" it meant sure death to someone within hearing, as much a threat to kill as if spoken in so many words.

For fifteen minutes Cherokee Bill gobbled and fired at every form he could see. He fired at Jim Shannon and another citizen as they were carrying Keating's remains outside. The place was redolent with the smoke of gunpowder. Only this and the fact that the officers were able to keep Cherokee confined in his cell prevented a dozen men from being slain.

Firearms were at every step. The prisoners, for the most part badly frightened, had taken refuge beneath their bunks or huddled in the corners of their cells. On the outside of the cell blocks were twenty or more men, all armed to the teeth. Captain Berry vainly tried to induce Cherokee to surrender his weapon. A steady refusal was the only response.

The crowd outside had assumed alarming proportions. The cry "Lynch him! Hang him!" was frequently heard. Vengeance boiled in many breasts. Keating was a popular citizen of Fort Smith and one of the oldest officers of the court. He had served as guard at the jail for nine years.

Cherokee Bill heard these shouts; he knew the temper of the mob, and feared he was about to be brought out to a terrible death. One word from Crump and swift, certain justice would have been meted out. He told the outlaw to surrender, that further fighting was useless.

Cherokee yelled back: "I didn't want to kill Keating; I wanted my liberty. Damn a man who won't fight for his liberty! If I hadn't shot him, he would have shot me."

Then he pleaded for the protection of the law that he had so many times outraged, and told the marshal, "If I could have captured the jail, no one would have been killed."

He signified no intention of giving up, however.

Starr watched from his north end cell on the west side. Though his door was open, he had made no demonstration. He called to Crump: "If you will promise not to kill Bill, I will go and get his pistol."

It was an unheard-of thing to do. The officers did not fancy his entering the badman's cell, but it appeared the only solution to their seemingly insoluble dilemma, and Crump believed in the sort of Freemasonry that existed among the Cherokees. He told his men to hold their fire.

"Shooting is too good for him," Crump ordered. "Save him for the gibbet."

What happened next is confused in history. The dime novelists compare Starr with a Christian gladiator entering the ring with a lion: "Unarmed, considerably smaller in physique, he nevertheless sprang at the murderous Goliath. There was a desperate man-to-man struggle, but in the end he subdued his powerful adversary. . . ."

Sutton,[5] drawing on his imagination, writes:

"Bill, you can't get anywhere by killing a lot of people. You can't get out now. Stop it and give up your gun," urged Starr.

"I'm going to kill every white man in sight, and if you don't hike out of range I'll kill you, too," Bill growled.

Starr had noticed that on several occasions when Cherokee's old mother came to see him, Bill had sat all the time with his arm around her. He loved his mother and she was probably the only person on earth he had any regard for. . . . Bill's soft spot was his love for his mother.

"Bill," called Starr, "you know your mother wouldn't want you to kill any more than you've already killed. Don't make it any harder for her."

Bill handed his six-shooter to Starr and surrendered. . . .

W. B. Lawson[6] says no one ever knew how Starr persuaded the murderer to give up his weapon:

Without a word, he walked down the passage to Bill's cage, swung open the door and entered. The officers . . . listened attentively, but heard only a faint whispering. A moment later Starr stepped out . . . and delivered the badman's gun to the officers.

Drago[7] claims he was "released" from his cell; that he strode down the corridor "calling to Cherokee Bill," but "what passed between them will never be known" except it was something more than his laconic: "Bill, your mother wouldn't want you to do this. Give me your gun and call it quits."

This is contrary to Starr's version in *Thrilling Events:*[8] "I pledged myself to get Bill's gun if [Crump] would give me his word of honor that he would not shoot him when disarmed, which he did. I went at once to Bill's cell and told him that he could not possibly get out—that he might be able to kill a few more guards, but that would avail nothing, and to take my advice and give his gun to me, which he did, loaded all round. I walked to the end of the corridor and handed the gun to the guards."

It was that simple.

The officers entered the corridor, covering Cherokee with shotguns and Winchesters. A thorough search of his cell turned up a little tobacco sack filled with .38 cartridges. Then he was handcuffed, chained, and locked back inside. George Pearce, whom they found hiding in his cell, was also chained and locked up, and the jail cleared of spectators.[9]

The marshals and guards worked until midnight dispersing the crowds and discouraging mob violence. District Attorney Read mingled quietly with the people, assuring them the case would be vigorously prosecuted and the crime would not go unavenged. Nothing else was talked about in public places for a week, while Cherokee rattled his chains like an animal in captivity and Read moved swiftly to make good his promise.

The autumn term of court began on August 5. The trial docket, seldom taken up until October, was so heavy Judge Parker cancelled his vacation, which he usually took at this time of year. For the first time in the court's history the petit and grand juries were empaneled on the opening day. There were twenty-five murder cases scheduled, and the grand jury added a dozen more. The first case taken up was the killing of Keating.

The judge's charge to the grand jury was very forceful. Within half an hour they returned an indictment against Cherokee Bill, and at 1 o'clock in the afternoon, escorted by a dozen armed deputies and a court bailiff with a heavy billy, he was arraigned before Parker. He entered a plea of not guilty, and Parker set his trial for August 8.

Until that time it had been impossible for the District Attorney and his able assistant, McDonough, to obtain any information as to the instigators of the plot resulting in Keating's murder. The indictment of Cherokee Bill alone caused the prisoners to think no others would be involved, and some of them began talking. Before the grand jury adjourned, it handed in new indictments against Starr, Sherman Vann, George and John Pearce, Ed and John Shelley, and Ed's wife Lou. Several others in Murderers' Row became witnesses against them. Cherokee Bill denied that any of them had a part in the plot. He swore that Ben Howell, a trusty who had run away July 1, had brought both revolvers in to him on June 27, and that he and Buz Luckey were to have done the fighting for possession of the jail. His statement was not believed. Vann already had admitted bringing in the bucket in which the revolver had been found on July 10, and "there was other evidence tending to show Mrs. Shelley had carried the second revolver in to her husband wrapped in a shawl." Assistant District Attorney McDonough also pointed to the fact that Buz Luckey was in Cell Number 24, his door locked, and the person responsible for throwing the "brake" that started Bill and George Pearce on their rampage had to be someone near the north end of the west row of cells. He named Henry Starr, but "none saw him in the act." [10]

All pleaded not guilty. Starr and Pearce were brought

into court handcuffed together. The handcuffs were removed from the others, but Starr and Pearce stood in irons while arraigned. The prisoners had no attorneys when brought in, and Clayton and James Brizzolara, former prosecutor for the city of Fort Smith, were appointed to defend them. The attorneys objected to Starr and Pearce being chained, and Judge Parker replied:

"Make your objections in writing. The court is very willing to grant the prisoners all the privileges they are entitled to, but it does not propose to sit here and endanger its life as well as the lives of the innocent spectators in the courtroom."

The attorneys also excepted to his remarks on the ground that they were made in the presence of the petit jury that was soon to try Starr for the murder of Floyd Wilson.[11]

"The low cunning of the assistant prosecutor was again shown," Starr said.[12] "No doubt he and the judge had their heads together, and smarting under the sting of the Supreme Court's rebuke, decided to play their trump card. . . . The guards and officials at the jail were furious and promised that I should get the best of it. Such dastardly action was bound to react. . . ."

The indictment was finally nol-prossed. But this was after Cherokee Bill had been convicted of Keating's murder. Parker sentenced him to be hanged on September 10. Cherokee again appealed to the Supreme Court, and the judge issued another stay of execution. On December 2, the Supreme Court affirmed the decision of the Fort Smith court in the Ernest Melton case, and for the third and last time Judge Parker sentenced Cherokee Bill to the gallows. He was hanged on St. Patrick's day, March 17, 1896.

Starr's new trial for the murder of Wilson began on September 15, 1895. The evidence was practically the same. Starr feared nothing more than a conviction of manslaughter. "He went on the stand and corroborated the most damaging testimony against himself, admitting that he advanced on Wilson all the time and was standing almost over his prostrate body when the fatal shot was fired into Wilson's breast," [13] and again pleaded self-defense.

"The wicked flee when no man pursueth, but the righteous are as bold as a lion," charged the implacable, white-haired Parker, and instructed the jury: "The law says that a man is to be judged by his consciousness of the right or wrong of what he does. . . . If he flees from justice because of that act, if he goes to a distant country, and is living under an assumed name . . . living so as to conceal himself . . . because of that fact, the law says that is not in harmony with what innocent men do, and jurors have a right to consider it as an evidence of guilt . . . the law says you have a right to take that fact into consideration as one from which you may infer guilt—a presumption of fact . . . a silent admission by the defendant that he is unwilling or unable to face the case against him. It is, in some sense . . . a confession, and it comes in with other incidents, the corpus delicti being proved, from which guilt may be cumulatively inferred." [14] Again Starr was convicted of murder and sentenced to die.

Once more he appealed to the Supreme Court. "Fatally defective," wrote Mr. Justice Edward D. White. The weight to be given evidence of the flight of the accused, as stated by the trial court to the jury for their guidance, was, at the most, "slight." Flight did not raise a "legal presumption" or "inference of guilt," but was only one of the series of circumstances to be considered by the jury with the reasons that prompted it. The conviction was set aside, with directions to grant a new trial.[15] Strange to say, the court in later years departed from this rule and upheld instructions in criminal cases containing substantially the same language as used by Parker. In Oklahoma flight has been held a circumstance tending to prove guilt in many cases.[16]

The opinion was handed down on January 4, 1897. This was after the death of Judge Parker on November 17, 1896, a little more than two months after Congress had seen fit to reduce his court from the greatest criminal tribunal in history to one of comparatively petty jurisdiction over a handful of counties in western Arkansas.

"Judge Parker was no doubt an able man, and of extensive legal learning," Starr said, in *Thrilling Events*.[17] "But he had fought evil-doers so long that even those closest to him admitted he was a monomaniac on the subject of crime. I can scarcely take so charitable a view of the judge because he conspired to convict Alf Cheney when the densest mind in the court room could see that he was wholly innocent. . . . After I again took my case to the Supreme Court, Judge Parker had a newspaper controversy with Justice White. Justice White flayed his honor of Fort Smith for flagrant abuse of power, and Parker replied, charging Justice White with a lack of knowledge of the law. Right then Judge Parker got in bad, and for him to say that a Justice of the U. S. Supreme Court knew nothing of the law is a striking example of this man's bigotry and exaggerated ego. I don't pretend to be on the inside, but have a sneaking suspicion that friends of the offended Justice got the ear of Congress and that body promptly and effectively stripped the Honorable Isaac Parker of his kingly power by taking the Indian Territory from his jurisdiction. They cut off his tail close up—bully for Congress. . . .

"How our good old Uncle Sam got stuck up, shook down, and double crossed by that court at Fort Smith! Court never adjourned—one term ran on 'til another was due, and let it also be remembered that witnesses came as far as 300 miles and received mileage and $1.50 per day for expenses while at court. A marshal got so much per witness subpoenaed, and not one witness out of every four was used, while often 30 or 40 in one case would remain two months, and then the case would be continued. If tried, not one out of five knew a material fact. Of course we could expect a host of professional witnesses; the same men were called from term to term, stool pigeons of the deputy marshals, haunting the saloons and low dives which flourished and grew fat in Fort Smith. Naturally this swarm of witnesses promoted such industries as saloons and houses of ill-fame, and cheap boarding houses.

"It is not my intention or desire to cast the remotest reflections upon the good citizens of Fort Smith; far from it, for during my stay there in durance vile, of four years and six months, I came to know most everybody in town; and I would be an ungrateful wretch indeed if I failed to remember and be thankful for the many kindly favors and expressions of sympathy and cheer proffered by many of the best citizens, who loved fair play and knew my case was one of 18 karat shanghai. I stayed so long that these good people almost looked upon me as a native son. I wish to add that the guards and keepers treated me with the greatest consideration, and were always willing to do me a favor. I spent most of my time during those long years reading good books supplied by my attorneys and friends, and was also allowed all and any newspapers and periodicals, and I bought many. [Starr formed the habit of writing articles to the newspapers, and many of these were published in the Fort Smith *Weekly Elevator*.] I was eager for knowledge. I figured if they did hang me, the information acquired wouldn't make their job any easier, and if they didn't, such knowledge would help me earn an honest living when they released me.

"Soon after Congress took the jurisdiction of Indian Territory from Fort Smith . . . Judge Parker was no more, and the gang of fawning syncophants, true to their hyena instincts, sneaked away when they should have stayed to cheer and condole. But such action is as old as history; Kings and Emperors have experienced the same requiescat in pace. The leading business men saw that the town had a commercial future, and wished the bloody past to be obliterated. Senator Vest of Missouri, in a speech on the floor of the senate, said that the place was a shambles, a butcher's domain, a stench and a disgrace to civilization and humanity. The old gallows which had for so long been one of the show places of the town, and the fort's walls, were removed in January, 1898. Hon. John R. Rogers, a former member of Congress from Arkansas, was appointed to fill the place of Judge Parker, and soon disposed of all criminal cases pending."

Starr's case was among these. On October 6, 1897, he entered a plea of guilty to manslaughter, and on January 15, 1898, was sentenced to three years in the penitentiary at Columbus, Ohio.[18] He already had been convicted on seven counts of robbery, for which he drew seven years and seven days.[19] In addition, he was given five years for the Pryor Creek affair, making a total imprisonment of 15 years and seven days.[20]

Judge Rogers gave him a "kind and fatherly" talk. His conduct during his residence in "Parker's Hotel" indicated a desire to become a decent citizen, and if his future actions were as exemplary, the court would, in a reasonable time, join in recommending a full pardon.

"On January 23," Starr wrote,[21] "I left Fort Smith to begin my sentence. I withstood the sudden change from the sunny South to the cold and frozen North in the dead of winter remarkably well, but many of the poor fellows from the Indian Territory succumbed to the rigorous climate and hard work put upon them. There were over 500 United States prisoners in Columbus at the time I entered. I had my neck bowed to do that sentence and do it well, irrespective of conditions, and my record as a prisoner was perfect; only the rankest fools and imbeciles give trouble in prison. Hon. E. G. Coffin was warden, and through the intercession of friends, granted me many important privileges.

"My sentence read that no part of it should be spent at hard labor, and my work was piece-meal and easy. I learned the trade of glovemaker and after two years of steady work was considered, by outside men who knew, to be competent to work in any shop. I also worked as assistant butcher and bread-cutter."

Starr also convinced prison officials and his friends in the Indian Territory that he had reformed. His mother made numerous efforts to obtain his release, without success. In the fall of 1901, through Colonel William M. Cravens, then practicing law at Muskogee, she appeared before the Cherokee National Council at Tahlequah.[22] The proceedings appear in Cherokee Volume 312, page 275,

Senate Journal, Regular Session, Senate Chamber, 2 o'clock P.M., Friday, November 29:

. . . Senator Mayes presented a Resolution asking for an unconditional pardon of Henry Starr now confined in the penitentiary at Columbus, Ohio, and asked that same be read. Resolution read.

Senator Mayes moved that the rules be suspended and that the resolution asking for the pardon of Henry Starr be considered on its second reading. Resolution was so considered.

Senator Morgan moved that the resolution asking for the pardon of Henry Starr be placed on its passage. Vote taken. Resolution passed. . . .

The wording was, in part, as follows:

Whereas, about the first of July, Eighteen Hundred and Ninety Three, Henry Starr a Cherokee Indian Boy was arrested and imprisoned in the United States jail Fort Smith, Arkansas, upon the charge of murder in killing Floyd Wilson and upon charges of robbery alleged to have been committed in the Cherokee Nation . . . and was sentenced to imprisonment in the penitentiary at Columbus, Ohio . . . for fifteen years and seven days.

On these charges he has been in prison for more than eight years. At the time of his arrest he was only nineteen years of age. He was born of highly respected and honored parents, was an intelligent and high spirited boy, and during his imprisonment, instead of choosing his associates among the demoralized and vicious, he showed a disposition to improve himself, and during his long confinement in jail from July, Eighteen Hundred and Ninety Three, to January, Eighteen Hundred and Ninety Eight, he was encouraged by his lawyers and others to study and educate himself, and was furnished with good books, and read and acquired a fair education.

By his honorable and gentlemanly conduct in jail he won the confidence of all the officers of the jail and court, by his timely advice and information to the officers of the jail on more than one occasion assisted in preventing seriously threatened riots and bloodshed.

When about Seventeen years of age by a course of unfriendly persecution he felt himself driven to leave home and go upon the scout, and while so scouting killed Floyd Wilson and was charged with said robberies.

As to the killing of Floyd Wilson, the testimony, if it did not show that he was justifyable [*sic*], left the question in great doubt.

As to the robberies charged, Henry was a boy when they were alleged to have been committed and fell in with badmen also on the scout, and while so scouting killing Floyd Wilson and was charged with said robberies.

And now for more than Eight years both in jail at Fort Smith, Arkansas, and at the penitentiary at Columbus, Ohio, he has shown himself to be a reformed man, and of that character which will make a good, honest, and useful citizen.

Therefore, be it resolved by the National Council of the Cherokee Nation, that the President of the United States be respectfully but earnestly requested to grant him an unconditional pardon.

143

Concurred in by the Council
Nov 29—1901.
    E. S. SHELTON
    Clerk of Council

Approved Nov 30—1901
    T. W. BUFFINGTON
    Principal Chief [23]

The following spring, with this resolution and a score of testimonials and affidavits, Starr's mother journeyed to Washington and placed her son's case before President Theodore Roosevelt.[24] Roosevelt, always an admirer of masculine courage and virility, was so impressed with the story of how Starr had taken the gun from Cherokee Bill that he wired Henry in prison: "Will you be good if I set you free?"

Starr promised, and the President commuted his fifteen-year sentence to expire January 16, 1903.[25]

IX

Back to the Bandit Trail

Clicking telegraph keys spread the news. Border newspapers carried such headlines as "Once Notorious Outlaw Released From Prison"; "Promises He Will Be Good"; "Pardoned After Nine Years, He Will Endeavor to Repay His Mother's Devotion." In connection with the latter, the Tulsa *Democrat*, of January 20, 1903, printed this brief item:

Starr arrived here today with his mother. It is said upon good authority that she has spent $6,000 in various efforts in his behalf. He certainly owes her a great deal. The mother now runs a restaurant in Tulsa. Starr says he will pursue the way of peace, and indicates that he will assist his mother in business.

Henry worked in the restaurant only a few months. In

145

September, he married Miss Ollie Griffin, "a part Cherokee, and a girl of much refinement and culture." [1]

According to Representative Walter R. Eaton of Muskogee, Miss Griffin was a schoolteacher and was boarding
at the Starr home in the autumn of 1902, at the time Eaton
was engaged in promoting the townsite of Porum, thirty
miles south of Muskogee on the Midland Valley railroad.
Eaton was going through the country with a photographer,
getting pictures with which to advertise the section. Late
one evening, while driving by the home of Henry's mother,
they spotted a very pretty young woman milking a cow
in the barnyard. "The entire scene was one to capture our
fancy," Eaton recalled, "and we finally persuaded her to
pose for us. We got several fine pictures, one of which we
labeled 'The Cherokee Milkmaid.' It attracted instant attention because of its artistic merits and was published
throughout the United States in magazines and newspapers. About a year later, this young woman married
Starr." [2]

On May 27, 1904, the Vinita *Daily Chieftain* reported:

Henry Starr, one of the most noted ex-outlaws of the
Cherokee Nation, has settled down and become an excellent citizen. . . . He appeared at the Tahlequah
land office today to file on an allotment for himself, his
mother and his wife and sister. All the family took allot-
ments in a body near Tulsa, and it is a fine piece of
property.

Shortly afterward, Henry's wife gave birth to his "only
son and heir," whom he named Theodore Roosevelt, in
honor of the president who had freed him.

"I engaged in the real estate business around Tulsa,"

Starr wrote,[3] "and resided there until 1907; then we moved to the small town of Skiatook, only six miles from my allotment. This was the year Oklahoma became a state, and I took my wife and young Ted to the inauguration of Hon. C. N. Haskell. . . . It was a perfect day—just enough of the military to lend color to the scene. Crack bands from all over were there at their best, and the crowds were in gala attire. We made our way to the Carnegie Library where the inaugural exercises were to be held, myself and family standing near the front where the governor and party would stand. As he stepped forward to take the oath of office and deliver his address, I held my small son high above the crowd to see the first governor of Oklahoma. Although not of the same politics, I had voted for Haskell because the Republicans had the effrontery to ask decent people to vote for a carpetbagger, and I had had enough of that tribe. And when Governor Haskell spoke so feelingly of the state's duty to the Indians and gave the Indian Orphan Band the place of honor in the parade at the exercises later in the day, I was glad I had voted for him; racial pride and welfare triumphed over political faith. In addition, Robert L. Owen, himself a Cherokee, took the oath of office as U. S. Senator from Oklahoma; and all around the Governor and his party were dark-haired men and women, prima-facie evidence that the Redman intended to help guide the ship of state. I'll admit I went away feeling rather proud and chesty, for I was living an honest, upright life—proud of my home and family, and interested in all things pertaining to the welfare of my fellow man. . . . A few days later I learned that the state of Arkansas had made requisition to the Governor of Oklahoma for my person for robbing the Bentonville bank in June, over 13 years before."

Bentonville authorities had kept the old indictment alive. Shortly after Starr's release from prison, they had tried to extradite him, but the officials of the Cherokee Nation had refused, claiming such a course of retaliation for the refusal of the state of Arkansas to honor Cherokee requisitions. So the Bentonville authorities had waited, watching Henry as a cat would a mouse. With the Cherokee Nation now a part of Oklahoma, and Henry a citizen of the new state, would Governor Haskell honor their application?

"I sent a friend to the governor," Starr said,[4] "to tell him how for five years I had been going straight, and to beg him not to let the wolves get me. I did not know what the governor might do, and having some experience with hill-billy juries and feeling that a community that would hound a man for a past offense after years of proper conduct could scarcely be expected to give him justice, I took to the tall and uncut. I was determined not to go to Arkansas. I preferred a quiet and unostentatious interment in a respectable cemetery rather than life on a convict farm where the lash and bloodhound were the primary accessories of gentle persuasion. . . . For two months I hid out at the home of a friend in the Osage hills. Imagine my humiliation and utter dejection when I learned that Governor Haskell had absolutely refused to give me up. . . . [The governor had turned down the application upon the opinion from the attorney general that there was no authority for extraditing members of the Five Civilized Tribes to a state or territory for a crime less than murder.]

"This period of my life I shall always be ashamed of; I betrayed the confidence of my friend and the governor. All past wrongs seemed to rise up and cloud my better judgment. My reason seemed to leave me, and I simply went to pieces. Had I stayed to face the music, I might still hold a place of honor and respect with my people. . . . Instead, during the fall and winter of 1907 and the early part of 1908, two banks were robbed in Kansas and Missouri, and two in Oklahoma—all happened in the daytime and within a few days of each other, and the papers credited me with having again got off the reservation with forty kinds of war paint on. Of course we must always allow our newspaper friends considerable latitude. Hell had broke loose, and somebody had to be charged with the crimes; what more natural than that I should be the fall guy, since I was the only man loose who could rob a bank, and my whereabouts unknown? The same old story of giving a dog a bad name.

"The papers claimed I was in all of them and had me in four different places at the same time. Special correspondents were rushed to the scenes and large bodies of armed men were supposed to be close on my trail. I deny these charges in toto, and in three of these cases the bandits have since been apprehended and convicted. . . ."

Actually, Starr had teamed up again with his old pal Kid Wilson, who, by that time, had been paroled from Brooklyn, New York, and returned to their old haunts in the Osage. They were seen often during the winter "hanging around" Bartlesville. Starr's family remained in Skiatook. Toward the end of February, they purchased two Winchester rifles and five hundred rounds of ammunition from a Bartlesville man named Clark, and rode north. On Friday afternoon, March 13, 1908, they crossed the Oklahoma border into Tyro, Kansas, "where the principal amusement was watching the four o'clock Santa Fe train come in," robbed the State Bank of $2,500, and set off a countryside manhunt.

The story of their sixty-hour flight through the old Cherokee and Osage nations appears in the Bartlesville *Daily Enterprise*, March 16:

From Tyro, the bandits started due south. Deputy Sheriff Amik and Mr. Dabney were the first to leave Tyro in pursuit and others caught up with them before they had gone ten miles. By the time the party had reached Wann, the Tyro posse numbered twenty men. Posses started from Deering and from Caney, and before evening the roads were covered with men in pursuit of the desperadoes.

The first "brush" between the bandits and the Tyro posse took place in a creek hollow two miles north of Wann. It was thought they had the outlaws surrounded. Men were coming from the south from Wann and others were approaching from the east. The Tyro posse rode straight ahead.

But they were mistaken . . . the bandits opened fire from the edge of the woods . . . the horses were shot from under Amik and Dabney. This checked the progress of the pursuit . . . the bandits waved their hats on their rifles, gave a warwhoop and rode southwest.

An effort had been made meanwhile to organize a posse at Wann with little success. Leonard Lee, city marshal, and Lee Doncarlcon started northwest to head off the bandits. Lee had only his six-shooter and Doncarlcon only a few shells for his gun, so neither could do very effective work in checking the bandits' progress. From the top of a hill they saw the outlaws coming.

Twenty shots were fired, and finally a bullet hit Marshal Lee, knocking the revolver from his hand and passing through his hand under the bones.

As soon as Lee had been shot he ran to a nearby house, the robbers continuing in his direction. Lee thought that they were following him and ran upstairs. He told the woman of the house to be level headed and not to act frightened, that if the men tried to come upstairs he would kill them. The bandits rode up to the house . . . but did not molest either the man upstairs or the woman . . . and proceeded on their way.

The Tyro aggregation meanwhile had mustered their nerve, patched up their losses and come on in the direction of Wann. The marshal had lost his pocketbook on the crest of the hill and a Wann man was sent after it. He rode down the highway; the Tyro bunch could be seen about a quarter of a mile away. Thirsting for blood, they were intent on shooting everything in sight. They opened on the reconnoitering party from Wann. The man waved his arms and tried to show that he was a friend, but the Tyro posse shot all the faster. The man turned his horse and rode at a hot pace back to town. Further on the aggregation came upon another Wann man in a buggy going home and opened fire on him from the rear. Rather elderly and unused to such familiarity . . . he did not stop to find out whether they were friends or foes. He whipped up his horse and pulled away from his assailants. It was reported at Wann that the "natives" all along the road were out with corn knives and shotguns and that it would indeed be dangerous for a stranger to make his way along the highways after the sun had set. Behind every fence post and in every clump of weeds there lingered one man or a dozen ready to shoot down a bank robber or peaceable citizen without the least provocation.

The excitement increased as the robbers moved southwest from Ochelata. The *Enterprise* report continues:

The men reached that part of the country Sunday morning. Immediately the women living along the rural telephone line became interested and began informing the authorities of the movements of the bandits.

"The outlaws have just stopped on a hill above our house," one woman telephoned to the central office. After an interval of thirty minutes, another rang central and said: "The bank robbers just stopped here and asked for a drink of water."

So it went during the entire time the men were making their way into the Osage. The authorities followed these telephone directions as best they could, but only one posse saw them yesterday. . . .

This posse went out from Ochelata and was composed of Joe Daniels, Rock Flannigan, A. P. Tullock and Monroe Staggs. Daniels, who is constable at Ochelata, and knows Starr, and Tullock, who also knows him, were discussing the probability that it was Starr and Kid Wilson they were hunting. It was 11 o'clock in the morning. . . . They had no thought of being close to their quarry . . . when suddenly a man stepped out to one side of a tent on an oil lease 100 yards ahead and began to motion them to go back.

The man was Wyatt, a camp cook. He had been ordered to cook breakfast for the outlaws. He saw the posse coming and thought he could prevent their capture by warning them of their danger, but they apparently did not know what the waving meant until Starr advanced from his hiding place beside the road with his rifle in his hands and called on the hunters to throw up their hands, and asked:

"What do you fellows want?"

One of the men had his pack of dogs with him and a horn hanging beside his saddle. Daniels took his cue from this and said:

"Why we have been wolf hunting and are just looking for a little bob-tailed hound of mine. You haven't seen him anywhere, have you?"

"Damn you and your bob-tailed hound," snarled Starr. "You are looking for me and you know it. Get their guns. . . ."

The second bandit stripped the arsenal from the captives while Starr stood guard. The guns were then broken on some rocks and their remnants returned to the men. Tullock had been a member of a posse which trailed Starr once before and the outlaw had sworn to kill him if he ever caught him under similar circumstances.

"I've got a notion to kill you," he told Tullock.

"Don't do that, Henry, without giving him a chance," said Starr's companion.

"I guess you are right," replied Starr; "just give him your gun and I'll fight it out with him."

This proposition didn't appeal to Tullock and he pleaded to be let go. Starr consented reluctantly. He then ordered one of his pursuers to dismount and take the saddle from his horse. The outlaws took this horse and gave a badly exhausted sorrel in exchange.

After the bloodless encounter Starr returned to the tent where he had ordered breakfast and asked that the food be wrapped so it could be carried. Taking this with them the men started on west. That was at noon and the last seen of them was about sundown last night, preparing to proceed into the hills along Hominy creek where Starr is familiar with the ground and where they will be safe from capture unless by a large well-organized force. . . .

The *Enterprise* doubted that such a force would be sent for them:

None of the manhunters here are familiar with the Hominy country and they would accomplish little on a hunt of that kind except to fall into a trap set by the outlaws. John Bird, sheriff of Osage county, is reported preparing for a trip after Starr . . . but rewards for these men aggregate only $800 a head, all are for "arrest and conviction," and not very enticing to the old manhunters of the Indian Territory country who do their best work when the offer reads "dead or alive."

Apparently Kansas, Montgomery county and insurance company officials took note. They upped the rewards for the robbers and offered them on a "dead or alive" basis. During the first week of April, circulars explaining the conditions and various amounts were posted throughout the country:

$2,450 REWARD

HENRY STARR: Age 37; height 5 ft. 9¾ inches; weight 170 lbs; spare build; straight and muscular; dark hair and eyes; high cheekbones; smooth shaven; is one-quarter Cherokee.

KID WILSON: Age 37; height 5 ft. 4 inches; weight 160 lbs; stout build; brown hair and eyes; smooth shaven; can raise brown beard; has scar on back of head and one right side of back as though from buckshot.

Rewards are offered as follows:

$1,500—The bank burgular insurance companies will pay $750 each for the apprehension and delivery to the sheriff of Montgomery county, Kan., of the said Henry Starr and Kid Wilson within ninety days from this date. If within ninety days from this date the said Starr and Wilson or either of them *are killed while resisting arrest for this crime,* the said reward of $750 each shall be payable upon satisfactory proof and identification of the body or bodies. Payment will be made through the representative of the companies, Ralph F. Potter, 122 Monroe Street, Chicago, Illinois.

$250—The governor of Kansas by proclamation dated March 31, 1908, offers a reward of $250 for the arrest within ninety days from that date and the final conviction thereof the unknown person or persons who committed this crime. Said reward to be paid upon such final conviction. Payment will be made by the proper state authorities.

$200—The Kansas Bankers' Association offers $100 each for the sheriff of Montgomery county, Kan., within ninety days from this date, of the above described Henry Starr and Kid Wilson. This reward is offered *upon the same terms as that made by the bank burglary insurance companies.* Payment will be made through W. W. Bowman, secretary, Kansas Bankers' Association, Topeka, Kansas.

$200—The board of county commissioners of Montgomery county, Kan., will pay $200 for the arrest and conviction of the criminals. The exact terms of this offer can be learned by addressing the county clerk, Independence, Kansas.

$200—The sheriff of Montgomery county, Kansas, offers $200 for the arrest and conviction of the criminals. The exact terms of this offer can be learned by addressing him at Independence, Kansas.

$100—The Tyro State Bank will pay $50 each for the apprehension and delivery to the sheriff of Montgomery county, Kansas, within ninety days from this date, of the said Henry Starr and Kid Wilson. Payment will be made by the bank *under the same terms as above detailed for the insurance companies.*

Meanwhile, Starr attempted to negotiate, through Tulsa friends, his surrender to the state authorities of Oklahoma. He was willing to give up, but he wanted Governor Haskell to guarantee that he would not be "dragged to other states" where he was not known and "detectives would try to convict him." He denied having participated in the robberies in Kansas, Oklahoma, and Missouri; even declared he "never had a hand in the Tyro job," and offered to furnish proof of his whereabouts at the time it was committed. He offered to meet a representative of the Governor at any place the latter might select, if promised protection. But Governor Haskell "refused to consider his proposition under the terms set forth." [5]

"In April, 1908," Starr wrote,[6] "I left Oklahoma on horseback in company with [Kid Wilson]. Our start was made near Muskogee, and we rode about 50 miles that day. The next day we stayed in the Creek country. This was about three weeks after the big uproar [Haskell's rejection of the terms of his surrender], and we were both carrying a rifle apiece and a .45 Colt's. The second night we made a light ride, and the grass being short, I invaded a farmer's corn bin. The third night put us out of the country where people knew me, and we decided to ride the balance of the trip in daylight. The third morning at sunrise we were . . . close to a pretentious looking dwelling and huge red barns about 12 miles north and 10 miles west of Oklahoma City, one of the finest farming countries I ever saw.

"As we approached the house, out came a typical Oklahoma boomer of about fifty, white hat awry; he wore a heavy mustache tinged with gray, and there were innumerable wrinkles around the shrewd, kindly blue eyes. He wore blue overalls and top boots, and a flannel shirt open at the throat; as fine a type of manhood as I ever had seen in my life, and worthy of the painter's best efforts. 'Fall off, boys,' said he, without asking names or where from, and as we dismounted, he walked to the kitchen door and bellowed: 'Two more for breakfast, mother, and hungry ones too, if I'm a judge.' For genuine unaffected, all-wool and a yard wide hospitality this Oklahoman may be equaled, but not surpassed. We spent a pleasant two hours with our boomer friend and his family. . . . Noon that day found us at another farmer's house and he was equally hospitable; we sat down to a fine chicken dinner, and after the repast were regaled with piano music by one of the farmer's charming daughters. That night we put up some miles west of El Reno at another farm house. The next day we crossed the South Canadian River into the Caddo Reservation, a rather hilly country. We never missed a meal and everywhere we went we were cordially welcomed. We continued our journey . . . north about 200 miles . . . and after four days' ride . . . were in that little strip known as 'No Man's Land,' but I want to tell you that it is filled with No. 1 people.

"The next few days brought us into New Mexico, where we stayed with a friend a month and a half. Late in June we came to Colorado and pulled off the Amity affair. . . ."

Amity, an isolated community in Prowers county, lay about ten miles west of the Colorado-Kansas border and twenty-five miles east of Lamar, above the Arkansas. Its bank, a small institution and completely unprotected, "looked too good to pass up." It was a "tame and featureless" robbery; Starr and Wilson paused just long enough to dip into its assets to the tune of $1,100, and escaped into the mountains. Even the pursuit was "amateurish." The nearest officers got to a hot trail was when they arrested a prominent cattleman living in the county who had known Starr previously in Oklahoma.[7]

After scouting several weeks in the mountains, the two bandits separated. Starr gives no reason for the parting in *Thrilling Events*, except that "Wilson wanted to quit for good" and rode off into oblivion. In speaking of the Kid to an old friend afterwards, he stated that he "grew to fear violence at Wilson's hands" and was "afraid Wilson was going nutty." [8] What happened to the diminutive outlaw remains one of the mysteries in Western history.

Starr spent the rest of the summer and the fall of 1908 near Tucumcari, New Mexico. "Nothing of note happened," he said.[9] "I rode a little every day to keep my horse in trim, practiced shooting with the same regularity, and occasionally tried my gun on antelope. . . . In January, 1909, I went from New Mexico to Arizona."

At Bosque, a little mining town in the Maricopa mountains southwest of Phoenix, he established residence under an assumed name. In Oklahoma, his wife, tiring of his absence and abortive efforts to become respectable, divorced him and moved to Dewey, three miles north of Bartlesville. Henry still had an interest in his Indian allotment, so he wrote a real estate man in Tulsa, whom he had known since childhood, to dispose of it and send him the money. The trust was misplaced:

"He told Fenton [S. W. Fenton, a state officer for Oklahoma] my Arizona address and alias. Fenton went to Colorado and brought the sheriff [John A. Simpson, of Prowers county] down with him, but stayed forty miles away [in Phoenix] while an Arizona officer [Wayne Davis, a local deputy sheriff] arrested me." [10]

The arrest occurred May 11. Starr at first denied his identity, but finally waived extradition. He left Arizona the morning of May 13 with Simpson and Fenton for Lamar, to be tried for the robbery at Amity.

"Of course, the newspapers got their usual food for big headlines," Starr wrote.[11] "The Colorado sheriff told how he and the detective leveled guns at my heart, and a lot of that stuff. . . . I understand Fenton got numerous promotions and credit for effecting my capture, and the sheriff, who had won his office by less than ten votes, got re-elected because of his ability to trail me all the way to Arizona. It's remarkable how such hypocrites get by. . . .

"I waived preliminary hearing and employed as counsel Hon. Granby Hillyer of Lamar. I have never regretted my selection for I regard him not only as a good lawyer but a conscientious gentleman. Again the sheriff showed his cowardly nature. Prowers county had just finished a new jail at great expense to the taxpayers, but for fear of the consequences if I escaped while under his care,

Mr. Cold Foot Simpson got an order from the court and had me transferred to Pueblo, with strict orders to let me see nobody. I was put in the solitary condemned cell and kept there from June 8th to November 24th and my bond fixed at such an exorbitant figure I had no chance to give. Several friends from Oklahoma came to Pueblo to see me, but were denied admission to the jail. . . . It didn't make any difference what I had done, they had no right to put me in solitary confinement before I had a trial; not apt to increase a man's respect for law and order nor that intangible thing they call society.

"I was brought to Lamar about the last of November and pleaded guilty. Received a sentence of from 7 to 25 years at Canon City, a very beautiful, charming summer resort, but not a nice place to go with a penal sentence hanging over your head.

"As I entered the prison a squarely-built man with a broad forehead and friendly eyes said, 'Henry, come over here. I want to talk to you.' His manner invited confidence; he introduced himself as the warden. We had two or three minutes' conversation. I felt that if a man treated Tynan square, he had nothing to fear. Thomas J. Tynan has done more practical good toward solving the great problem of penology than all the reformers of time. He starts while the men are under his care. He builds up their minds and bodies—you can't make a man better by harsh treatment, bad food and foul air. He appeals to their sense of fairness and manhood—his honor system long ago passed the experimental stage. Those who knocked now have to admit the warden knew what he was about. Seven states have adopted his system. It's easy to say 'Me too,' but it took a brave soul to say to the world: 'I'm going to give these poor fellows a chance.'

160

"A prisoner is allowed to go many miles, often 200, from the penitentiary without armed guards, to work on the roads. All between him and his liberty is his word not to run away. To the ordinary person it would seem a joke to send a man with many years to serve where he could walk away at will, but it's a fact that the percentage of runaways is so small as to be negligible. I worked on the road for over two years and the last sixteen months acted as night man of the camp, with a gun, horse and saddle at my disposal. To the average person who has gleaned opinion of me from newspaper writers it would mean murder, bank robbery and every crime in the calendar. Truth is, I stayed it out."

Besides serving as trusty in charge of a work gang, he studied law in the prison library, and officials declared he could have passed the state bar examination easily. He swore he had had enough, and in vindication of his past, wrote *Thrilling Events, Life of Henry Starr*. This autobiography was not published until more than a year later, but it brought his prison record to the attention of the pardon and parole board.

On September 24, 1913, he was paroled by the governor with the stipulation that he report once a month and never set foot outside the state of Colorado.[12]

X

The Most Banks Ever Robbed by One Man

Starr tried to stick to the terms of his parole. With permission of the state probation department, he journeyed back to Prowers county, where he had made a number of friends during his stay at Lamar. Already experienced in operating a restaurant, he opened a little short-order cafe at Holly, east of Amity and just four miles inside the Colorado border. But people were afraid of him and referred to him as "the bad man from Oklahoma." Business faltered. The pretty, brunette wife of a local merchant tried to help him. Starr's "magnetism won her favor," and Starr became infatuated with her. When the scandal broke, Starr closed his cafe, the woman deserted her husband, and they left Colorado together. Officials and detectives, who had been charged with keeping track of his movements, reported that Starr had returned to Arizona. Later, they learned he had been seen in Nevada.

Colorado made him a fugitive for parole violation—and the old bank robbery indictment at Bentonville was revived again.

Then, in the autumn of 1914, the first of the worst series of bank robberies in the Southwest occurred in Oklahoma. At two-week intervals, with clock-like regularity, one country bank after another was entered by one or two disguised men, who held up the officials or blew their safes and took the money in vaults and on counters.

Following is a list of fourteen banks robbed between September 8, 1914, and January 13, 1915: [1]

September	8—Keystone State Bank, $3,000
"	30—Kiefer Central Bank, $6,400
October	6—Farmers' National Bank of Tupelo, $800
"	14—Pontotoc Bank of Pontotoc, $1,100
"	20—Byars State Bank of Byars, $700
November	13—Farmers' State Bank of Glencoe, $2,400
"	20—Citizens' State Bank of Wardville, $800
December	16—Prue State Bank of Prue, $1,400
"	29—Carney State Bank of Carney, $2,853
January	4—Oklahoma State Bank of Preston ($1,200 damage to vault, no money taken)
"	5—First National Bank of Owasso, $1,500
"	12—First National Bank of Terlton, $1,800
"	12—Garber State Bank of Garber, $2,500
"	13—Vera State Bank of Vera, $1,300

These flagrant and successful daylight depredations left the state agape. The Southwest was shocked. Insurance companies threatened to cancel bank policies, and the harassed Oklahoma legislature, for the first time in its history, moved swiftly to pass a hurriedly drawn "bank-robber bill," appropriating $15,000 for the capture or death of "highwaymen and safe-blowers" and empowering the chief executive to place a price on the heads of bandits not to exceed $1,000 in any one case.[2]

Officers were unable to get a single clue. Detective agencies whose specialty was bank protection threw up their hands in despair. Then one of the victims in the Carney State Bank holdup of December 29 identified a photograph. In this equally brazen robbery, the bandits had been unmasked. According to the Chandler *News-Publicist*, of January 1, 1915:

. . . The men entered the bank, lined up the officials and several customers and pillaged the institution of all the currency they could find. . . . Contrary to all precedents they did not order their victims to "stick up their hands," instead they ordered them to keep their hands down, "For," remarked the coolest of the two, "we don't want to advertise this matter."

The affair was executed in a most methodical manner. One robber stood near the door while the other proceeded to keep order and get the coin. Cashier Austin was ordered to open the safe, but stated he did not know the combination. Immediately a six-shooter was shoved against his ribs and the order reiterated, with emphasis —Austin opened the safe. The robber made a careful search for money and secured, all told, about $2,500. . . . The men then marched their victims to the edge of town, entered a buggy (hitched in a grove of trees) and struck off across the country.

That evening they forced a farmer and his wife (north of Carney) to feed them, but since then have not been seen.

The leader of the pair, declared the bank cashier—and the farmer and his wife agreed—was Henry Starr.

On March 1, Governor Robert L. Williams issued his first proclamation under the provisions of the new bank-robber bill, which read, in part:

> Whereas, certain parties, one of whom is Henry Starr, are charged with the commission of said crime and are at large and have not been arrested . . .
>
> Now, therefore, I, R. L. Williams . . . by virtue of the authority vested in me by law, do hereby proclaim and offer that the state of Oklahoma will pay as a reward the sum of $1,000 for the arrest and conviction of said parties.
>
> It is further hereby proclaimed that in the offering of this reward, it is not contemplated that any life shall be taken, but if the said Henry Starr, or other of said parties while resisting arrest, is killed, upon the furnishing of satisfactory proof to me that he, the said Henry Starr, or other of said parties is guilty of the crime for which this reward is offered, the reward will be due and payable the same as if the said Starr or other of said parties had been arrested, tried and convicted.

The dead-or-alive clause was included primarily to "incite more effort" on the part of officers and serve as a warning to "any would-be bandits." But during the next three weeks, posses and individual manhunters made long scouting trips into the Osage hills, the brushy Bigheart mountains on the Cimarron, the Verdigris and Big Caney valleys in the old Cherokee Nation, and all the other haunts of Starr and his fellow longriders, with intent to kill, if necessary. They were convinced he was in Oklahoma, but they found no trace of him.

Meanwhile, Starr was engaged in one of the most daring maneuvers ever carried on by a fugitive from justice in America. In the heart of Tulsa, at 1534 East Second Street, he relaxed in a pretty five-room bungalow with electric lights, hot and cold water, bath and telephone, and "Laura Williams," the woman for whom he had violated his parole from the Colorado prison.

In a small garage at the rear of the property he kept a new five-passenger Dodge automobile in which he took nightly "joy rides" over the paved streets of the city. He was a regular patron of the local moving picture houses, where he saw enacted upon the silver screens reproductions of thrilling events suggestive of chapters in his own life.

He kept out of sight in the daytime, for within two blocks of the home lived Tulsa county's sheriff, Jim Wooley. Four blocks away lived Tulsa's mayor, Frank Wooden, and other close neighbors were members of the school board, newspapermen, and city and county employees who knew him intimately.

One block from his home was a newly erected church, and directly across the street, between Starr and the residence of Sheriff Wooley, was one of the city's largest ward schools. Each day scores of children played around the outlaw's back door at recess, and to his front door were delivered daily newspapers, whose columns were clamoring constantly for some sensational development in his checkered career.

166

No one thought of looking for him here. And the one- and two-man jobs that he could plan and execute so perfectly turned into a bigger dream. . . .

In the mail a few days later, Governor Williams received a letter that his confidential secretary, Arthur N. Leecraft, shoved aside as if the envelope contained a coral snake. On the stationery of a Reno, Nevada, hotel, appropriately dated March 16, it read:

"What do you and the legislature mean by having a $1,000 reward for me, dead or alive, for bank robbing? I did not know this reward was out for me until I met an Oklahoman here who told me. . . .

"Now, Governor, you surely have been misled, for I have not been in Oklahoma for years, and I can prove it by fifty men in Reno. They say you are a fair man, you will do square with anyone, and I hope you will be fair with me. I suppose I will be accused all my life, no matter if I am in Australia.

"Yours respectfully, Henry Starr."

Comparisons of known specimens of Starr's handwriting and the writing in the letter corresponded. The envelope, on close examination, however, showed a Tulsa postmark. It was later pronounced by state officials as a clever ruse of Starr's to turn suspicion away from him and his associates in the robbery of two banks in the same town on the same day and at the same hour—a feat no bandit gang in history had yet accomplished.[3]

The letter was received at the governor's office shortly after 9 A.M., Saturday, March 27, and exactly at that moment, seven men rode into Stroud, a prosperous little Lincoln county community on the Frisco, fourteen miles northeast of Chandler, and tied their horses at the stock-yards.[4]

One man stayed with the horses. The other six, led by Starr, split into two groups of three each and walked north to Main Street without arousing suspicion. No arms were in sight, and they were unmasked. Only one was disguised, wearing a gray wig and goggles.

The two groups reached Main Street a block apart, and signaling to one another, they entered the Stroud State Bank and the First National Bank simultaneously.

In the Stroud State Bank were Samuel Lee Patrick, vice president; J. B. Charles, Jr., bookkeeper; and J. M. Reed, a customer. Starr whipped out a short rifle he had carried under his coat shoved down the leg of his trousers, and his companions produced six-shooters. The drawers were quickly emptied of $1,600, and Starr ordered the bookkeeper to open the big safe, "or I will kill you."

"You will have to kill me, then," Charles replied. "I can't open it because I don't know the combination."

Starr turned to Patrick and said, "You know the combination, you open it."

Patrick told him the safe had been opened almost two hours earlier, the necessary money to operate the bank that day removed, and the time lock reset.

Starr pointed his rifle at Patrick's head. "I ought to pull the trigger," he said. At that moment, he noticed a diamond pin in Patrick's necktie. "This will make up some of the difference," he remarked, snatching the pin from the banker's tie and dropping it into his coat pocket. Then the robbers marched Patrick, Charles, and Reed out of the bank to join the second trio down the street.

The robbers at the First National were more successful. In his bank were President O. E. Grecian; H. E. Breeding, cashier; W. A. Chastain, bookkeeper; Claude Hood, clerk; and customers Joe Evans, H. M. Fendler, Charles L. Woods, and Julian Galloway.

"Who's the cashier?" asked one of the bandits.

"I am," replied Breeding.

"Get the money from the safe and give it to us," the bandit commanded.

Breeding sacked up the currency and silver amounting to $4,215.

"You men stand still a minute, and you won't be hurt," the bandits told the others. "We're waiting for our pals. They're robbing the other bank up the street."

When the trio saw Starr and his party saunter into the street, they ordered the First National officials and customers outside to join the parade. Marching their hostages before them, the two squads moved quickly, but without confusion, toward their horses.

Word of the holdups had spread, however. Townsmen rushed to vantage points, most of them too far removed for effective results, and began shooting with shotguns and revolvers. The robbers returned their fire, shooting promiscuously up and down the street to keep them from following and to clear away any opposition.

Despite the warning shots, the citizens continued to collect. Starr brought up the rear, using Banker Patrick as a shield. "Stand aside and let me get that bastard up there," he commanded Patrick, and aimed northward at Charles Guild, a horse buyer, who was coming around the corner with a double-barreled shotgun.

Starr fired one shot, the bullet piercing Guild's coat and singeing his vest. Guild hastily took cover. As Starr laughed, a rifle roared at him from the alley behind Brogan's meat market across the street. . . .

Paul Curry, a 17-year-old boy, who was standing in the back yard of his home 150 yards away, had seen the first trio leave the banks. He dashed into the butcher shop, grabbed up a sawed-off 30-30 Winchester rifle used for killing hogs, and ran to the rear of the store, taking a position behind some salt barrels. As Starr stepped from behind Patrick to shoot at the horse buyer, Curry fired.

The heavy slug struck the bandit leader in the left thigh below the hip, shattering the legbone and knocking him down. Temporarily paralyzed about the waist, he tried to return the fire. Curry threw another cartridge into the chamber of his hog rifle.

"Throw away that gun, or I'll kill you!" he shouted.

Starr tossed his weapon aside, and fell back on the ground.

Gaining courage from the excitement, the boy leaped from behind the barrels and made a beeline for the railroad tracks. The other outlaws had reached the stockyards with their hostages. All were mounting and riding off, except one, who was having trouble with a nervous horse. He was pulling at the reins and walking toward his fallen leader.

Curry fired again. The bullet struck the robber in the neck, breaking his left shoulder and injuring a lung. As his horse reared, he reeled and fell against the fence.

"Here," he called to Grecian and Cashier Breeding, "give me a hand."

At the point of a six-shooter, they helped him mount. He and the other five bandits rode rapidly to the southeast and disappeared in the blackjacks.

A mile and a half from town, the wounded robber began to lag behind. Weak from loss of blood, he fainted and fell off his horse. His companions took the animal and rode on, leaving him to his fate, as they had their leader, Henry Starr. He was soon found by a pursuing posse of armed citizens, who took him back to Stroud and laid him beside his chief.

As the gang disappeared, townsmen recovering from their panic had gathered around the bandit in the street. "I am Henry Starr," he said. At first they did not believe him, then recognized the "greatest outlaw of them all," for whose capture a $1,000 reward had been offered by the governor.

A hurried search of his clothing turned up a package of currency amounting to $1,100 and Patrick's diamond pin. These and his rifle were taken and men picked him up to carry him to a physician's office.

"Look out, they're coming back!" someone yelled.

The helpers dropped their load heavily to the sidewalk and scurried for shelter. But the alarm proved false, and Starr finally was carried to the office of Dr. John Evans over the First National Bank, where the second robber was brought a short time later and identified as Lewis Estes.

Estes refused to answer questions, but Starr told him he had "better tell where his parents lived" so they could be notified. He gave his address as Schalton, Missouri.

Evans attended both men's wounds. Starr displayed Indian stoicism, never whimpering as the doctor removed the rifle slug. Turning to the spectators, he asked: "What did the kid shoot me with?"

Told it was with a hog rifle, Starr commented: "I'll be damned. I don't mind getting shot, knew it had to happen sooner or later. But a kid with a hog gun—that hurts my pride!"

Later, he congratulated the youth for his remarkable

coolness and courage. Asked what he intended doing with the reward money, Curry replied that it would be used to pay for an education. "You are all right, boy," Starr said.

In gratefulness to Dr. Evans, Starr gave him the famous black horse he had ridden in so many raids. "He cost $500 but I won't be needing him," the outlaw added.

He apologized to Lee Patrick for "any inconvenience" he had caused him, and gave the banker his rifle.

And an enterprising photographer lugged his equipment to the doctor's office for a picture of Starr, which was circulated widely on postcards.

Sutton, in *Hands Up!* [5] writes that the people of Stroud wanted to hang Starr, and the bandit telephoned Bill Tilghman, the famous outlaw hunter and peace officer, at Oklahoma City to come protect him. Tilghman responded and "stopped the talk of lynching." Drago[6] accepts Sutton's story and states further, erroneously, that a "posse led by Tilghman surprised Starr's accomplices a few days later, and in the fight that followed, Lewis Estes *was killed*," two were captured, and the others escaped with the loot.

On the contrary, the following details appear in the Chandler *News-Publicist*, of April 2, 1915:

Even while the banks were being robbed news was 'phoned to Chandler and in just eleven minutes from the time the word came Sheriff George Arnold, Deputy Sheriff Hi Frisbie and several citizens were en route to the scene in automobiles. . . . Bill Tilghman did not hear of the robbery in time to *leave his home at Chandler* with the others, but went to Stroud later. . . . Arriving at Stroud a posse was organized and the chase after the fleeing bandits began.

County Attorney Streeter Speakman hastened to Stroud, and in answer to the demand for men and arms, arranged with Adjt. Gen. F. M. Canton for the use of the militia. Orders were 'phoned to Capt. H. B. Gilstrap, at Chandler, received by him 23 minutes before the train left. By train time he had eleven men armed with rifles and several hundred rounds of ammunition at the depot. Arriving at Stroud the men were loaded into automobiles and rushed to the hills.

This prompt action prevented the outlaws from reaching the Osage country, where, evidently, they were headed, and they obliged to keep closely under cover of the heavy timbered country. Men with rifles were dropped from the cars and ordered to scour the woods while the cars and a few armed men rushed to head off the outlaws.

Word was flashed to Bristow, Sapulpa, Okemah, Mounds, Drumright, Beggs and other points and from each place armed posses started out.

Soon came 'phone reports from where the outlaws had cut fences. The chase got warmer and warmer. At one time several cars were within 30 minutes from where the last wire was cut. The officers tried to hire or borrow horses so that they could trail the men across country, but in each instance the farmers refused to acede to the request. Had the officers secured horses the outlaws would undoubtedly have been captured, but without horses and night coming on, the chances of cornering the men were mighty slim. The chase was kept up, however, and several times the outlaws were forced to change direction and double back. At 11 o'clock Saturday night they cut the wire fence on the Jess Allen ranch and on the A. C. Smith farm, six or eight miles east of Bristow . . . headed toward Kelly-ville. This word was 'phoned over the country and Sunday morning the trail was picked up at the Smith place. It was followed for a couple of miles and found to have doubled back. This was the last trace secured. All day Sunday the militiamen on foot and officers and possemen in cars scoured the country without avail. It is practically certain that the outlaws found protection in the fastness of the hills and ravines east of Bristow. It is known that there are several "hold-outs" in that vicinity.

The Chandler officers, possemen and militia returned Monday morning, worn out and covered with mud and dust but satisfied that each had done his full duty.

The *Daily Oklahoman,* of Tuesday, March 30, added this item:

Three horses, all showing signs of a hard ride, were found tied in a clump of bushes a few miles from Kellyville Monday afternoon. That the horses belonged to the remaining members of the Starr gang is the belief of authorities. Jed Turner, 14-year-old son of a farmer living near Kellyville, says he saw four men walking through a field late Monday. He says they carried guns across their shoulders and he thought them members of a hunting party.

Sheriff Lew Wilder (of Creek county) went to Drumright and Oilton Monday and organized posses at each place to cut off all avenues of escape in that direction.

Saturday afternoon, Starr and Estes, guarded by Deputy Sheriff George Wilson and specially deputized citizens under the direction of County Attorney Speakman, were loaded aboard the westbound Frisco passenger train and taken to Chandler, where they were carried on cots to a hay wagon and driven from the depot to the jail. A crowd of seven hundred, attracted by the news of their arrival, escorted the wagon.

The Lincoln county jail consisted of an outside and inner cell in the basement of the courthouse, with iron bars and steel grating over the windows to keep ordinary prisoners from escaping. Solid steel doors gave entrances to the two cells. Starr and Estes were placed on cots in the outside cell with four other prisoners who were confined for petty offenses.

Dr. J. W. Adams administered anodynes to relieve the pain caused by rough jolting of train and wagon and redressed their wounds. Estes, a very sick man, lay without speaking.

With back and head supported by two pillows, Starr could talk face to face with officers and reporters without effort. "Under the thin blanket that covered him, his lean frame showed long, clean lines of muscle and bone. The enormous round chest was exposed by a gaping undershirt. He laid without restless movement of the hands. Both arms were stretched out easily and his face showed no sign of pain. The high cheekbones which betray his Cherokee blood were more prominent than usual as the result of fatigue and weakness. The eyes, deep in his head and wide apart, looked brightly at those about him. His voice was deep and steady as he calmly arranged for medical care and sending of messages to friends and relatives." [7]

Questioned about his crime life, Starr said it was all in *Thrilling Events,* already published. Asked about various

175

bank robberies in Oklahoma since his release from the Colorado prison, he admitted having a part in most of them, but shook his head as others were mentioned.

"Henry, why did you tackle the Stroud job with so many men when you have been getting by with only one partner or by yourself?" queried Deputy Wilson. "There's always some sucker in a gang of seven."

"They are all good hands. There isn't a sucker in the bunch," Starr replied, and glanced at Estes lying beside him.

When Undersheriff Brown asked who his companions were, Starr grinned, and Estes, who listened attentively but had nothing to say, closed his eyes and pretended to sleep.

Brown continued to needle Starr. If there were any "suckers" in the bunch, it was he and Estes. Estes had been the only man to attempt to ride back to rescue him; for that he had been shot, and after riding a short distance from town, the others had abandoned him, taking all the loot. Perhaps their pals weren't such "good hands" after all.

Starr could not be shaken. He was too old a head to say anything to either reporters or officers that would assist in the apprehension of his pals, and it already had been rumored that the gang would ride back, shoot up the town, and carry away the prisoners as soon as they were well enough to travel.

Brown assured him the town would prove a hard nut to crack. Besides, the sheriff's force would not be caught napping. Starr and Estes would remain in the special cell in the center of the courthouse basement surrounded by heavily armed guards until they were escorted to the pen.

Starr assured Brown that such security was unnecessary.

176

"I will go to prison this time without a fight," he said. His long career of crime had been brought to an end.

A heavy guard was kept on the jail, however, as Starr's friends and relatives poured into Chandler. Among these were the bandit leader's bent, gray-haired mother, and the "woman from Colorado" who insisted she was Starr's wife. Later, his friends tacitly admitted that she had been "living with him" in Tulsa. Starr identified her only as "Retta." She was permitted to enter his cell with his mother. All other visitors were barred.

At Tulsa, Sheriff Jim Wooley and his deputies searched the Starr house on East Second Street. The inside of the bungalow presented the general appearance of a modest American home. The windows were curtained, the floor carpeted, fancy work adorned the tables, and a Gramophone sat in the dining room. The record on the machine was titled "Where the River Shannon Flows." Slouch hats, cowboy boots, gauntlets, and work clothing that might have been used by either a highwayman or safeblower were strewn about the place, which had been left in an untidy condition when Starr's "wife" was hurriedly called to Chandler. A large quantity of ammunition for .45 Colt's revolvers and Starr's 35-caliber automatic rifle lay on the dresser.

The three horses left in the clump of bushes near Kellyville were brought to Sapulpa, and their descriptions sent to officers throughout the eastern part of the state and the Osage in an attempt to trace their ownership.

Meanwhile, County Attorney Speakman prepared for a vigorous prosecution of Starr and Estes. "Starr will be charged with conjoint robbery of the Stroud State Bank, which he entered and helped plunder," Speakman declared. "Estes will be charged with having helped rob the

177

First National Bank, and the separate informations will charge that the two men, cooperating with parties now unknown, also cooperated with one another in the robbing of the two banks. Both men were caught with the goods, both have practically acknowledged their complicity in the raid, and with a careful lookout for technicalities and a fair jury, they are billed for life terms."

Hard on the heels of this announcement came word that an effort was being made by state officials to connect Estes with the robbery of the Carney State Bank on December 29, and that Speakman was being importuned to use the information collected as the basis for a warrant charging him, with Starr, for that offense. When informed about the matter, Estes asked to see the county attorney, and Starr "got mad all over." [8]

What happened next is not clear. It was alleged that Estes agreed to turn state's evidence in the Stroud robberies in exchange for a "light sentence" and a promise that he would not be prosecuted for the Carney holdup. Other reports credited Starr with having been the first to turn informer and said that Estes was a tool of his at Starr's instigation. But it was Estes who "gave the names and residences of their pals."

On Wednesday night, March 31, Sheriff Wooley, upon information furnished by Sheriff Arnold of Lincoln county, arrested Bud Maxfield, a stock-raiser, near Turley, northeast of Tulsa. Maxfield was the robber who held the horses at the Stroud stockyards. The expedition had started from his home on Monday, March 22, and he had furnished some of the horses used by the gang.

On Thursday, April 8, Sheriff Arnold and Deputy Frank Miles located Claud Sawyer, "a tall, slim, fine looking young man," on his father's ranch near McAlester. In his

178

pockets when arrested was a "large sum of money" that contained a "certain stained $20 bill." Sawyer had entered the First National Bank with Estes, and was the man who had carried away the loot and taken Estes' horse after leaving Stroud.

Deputy Sheriff Hi Frisbie took the trail of the third alleged member of the gang, Charles Johnson, a prominent cattle buyer of Osage county. "All day Friday [April 9], during a heavy rain and wind storm, Frisbie and an Indian guide rode into the rough country east of Pawhuska —the hiding place of many an outlaw. Late Friday evening they found where Johnson had left his horse and saddle, and deciding that the rider would come for his property in the morning, camped there. About 6 A.M. Saturday, Johnson appeared and Hi flipped a six-shooter on him with the command 'stick 'em up.' Johnson obeyed orders and a search of his person brought to light a fine, new Luger automatic pistol, the very one that caused Lee Patrick to sit up and take notice that his bank was being robbed. Hi hurriedly caught a train, and, with his prisoner, arrived in Chandler at 7:30 Saturday night." [9]

The other members of the gang, identified by Estes as Joe Davis and Lige Higgons, men with long criminal records, fled into Arkansas and were never apprehended.[10]

On June 1, Starr and Estes were arraigned before County Judge H. M. Jarrett. Both appeared without counsel and waived preliminary hearing. They were bound over to district court under bonds of $15,000 each, which neither was able to furnish.

On July 19, Estes was arraigned before District Judge Charles B. Wilson, Jr. Again he declined counsel and entered a plea of guilty. Judge Wilson deferred sentence.

It was "no open secret" that Estes would take the

stand for the state and tell the whole story of the Stroud robberies. Defense attorneys for his pals charged that he had been promised immunity from prosecution in the Carney affair. The state denied it.

Sawyer was the first to be arraigned. "He appeared in court [July 20] dressed in a natty blue serge suit, white shirt and collar and carried one of his expensive sombreroes. He looked anything but an outlaw, member of a famous gang of dare-devils, which he is supposed to be." His trial was set for August 2nd, Johnson's for the 5th, Maxfield's for the 9th. "Starr, the acknowledged leader of the gang, has not yet been brought into court to plead. Starr does not know when he will be called upon. It all rests with the prosecution. Current opinion is that he will be allowed to remain quietly in his cell until after the trials of Sawyer, Johnson and Maxfield. It is rumored about town that he is to plead guilty when that time comes; that he will get a light sentence; and that he has been promised a parole by Governor Williams. Starr [has] emphatically denied this. . . . A large number of strangers are in Chandler expecting to attend the trials. Many are friends and former associates of the prisoners. Extra precautions are being taken by the sheriff's office to prevent any attempt at a jail delivery. Should such an attempt be made, the invaders will receive a hot reception." [11]

In a surprise move, on August 2, Starr appeared before Judge Wilson. He entered a plea of guilty and was sentenced to 25 years in the Oklahoma state penitentiary.

Immediately after Starr left the courtroom, Sawyer was put on trial for conjoint robbery. "From the very start the state wove a strong web about the defendant. Four bank officials and numerous citizens of Stroud positively identified Sawyer as one of the robbers of the First National.

People who saw the band as they were escaping swore that Sawyer was one of the bunch. The cashier of the bank identified the money found on him at the time of his arrest. And to cap the state's case, Lewis Estes, never batting an eyelash, took the stand and implicated Sawyer, Charley Johnson, Bud Maxfield, Henry Starr, Joe Davis and Lige Higgons." [12]

In his own defense, Sawyer attempted to prove an alibi. But he failed to convince a discerning jury of Lincoln county farmers. They brought in a verdict of guilty. He was sentenced to 5 years in prison. Maxfield, who offered no defense, was given 7 years.

In Johnson's trial, defense attorneys succeeded in getting Estes to "contradict himself many times," and his testimony "had little weight with the jury." Although numerous witnesses swore they "thought he was the man," the "disguise with a gray wig and goggles made positive identification doubtful." Johnson was acquitted. [13]

On Saturday, August 14, Judge Wilson passed sentence on Lewis Estes—five years at hard labor; and on Sunday morning, Sheriff Arnold, escorting him and Starr, boarded the train for McAlester. Maxfield and Sawyer, by counsel, filed notice of appeal. Their appeals failed to materialize, and on August 25, they were delivered to the state prison. [14]

XI

A Debtor to the Law

Starr's sentence turned out as all other sentences he had received. Almost at once his sharp wit went to work for him as never before. Again he lived up to the rules, worked in the library, taught classes in spelling and composition to other prisoners, and spent long hours assisting the chaplain in his duties. "This man has undoubtedly reformed," the chaplain told Warden A. B. Dick, in 1918. Thus the way was paved for another release.

A few months later, the attorney who had prosecuted him, most of the jurors who had convicted him, and the judge who had sentenced him were convinced that it was all a mistake!

The wound he received at Stroud had permanently crippled him. In recommending a parole for Starr, in February, 1919, Streeter Speakman said: "Considering his aged and crippled condition, I believe he will bring his career as a bank robber to a close as soon as he regains his freedom. He is a man of unusual intelligence. He is not a low, depraved type of humanity, and is capable of making a good citizen. . . ."

But it was Kate Barnard, Oklahoma's first commissioner of charities and corrections, who made her influence felt. She had more or less taken Starr as her personal project from the first day he landed behind the bars of the state prison.

A farm girl, who from childhood saw and studied first-hand the seamy side of life and resolved that her life would be devoted to aiding the poor and underprivileged, Miss Barnard had become known as one of the greatest humanitarians in the Southwest. In 1905, she converted her home in Oklahoma City into a distribution center for gifts to the poor by societies, clubs, and school children. Her charity work won such recognition that she was given an audience before the constitutional committee in January, 1907, and made an appeal for a provision to prevent child labor. Two months later, her battle won, she was presented the pen used to sign the article providing for a commissioner of charities, and immediately announced herself as Democratic candidate for the newly created office, to which she was elected.

This marked the beginning of a turbulent life for Kate Barnard. In April, 1908, she descended like an avenging fury upon amazed Oklahoma county officials because of what she termed "pest house horrors." Male nurses were caring for women patients in treatments that required baths and rubdowns. Her denunciations were so scathing that women nurses were installed and other reforms instituted. After a four-day investigation of the hospital for the insane at Norman, in January, 1910, Miss Barnard said: "Hell has reigned here 20 years undisturbed." She called for a change in administration.

In February, she asked Governor Haskell to submit legislation providing for jail sanitation. A year later she toured Oklahoma counties organizing conference charity groups, one objective being to enforce compulsory education. At the same time the legislature looked with favor upon her proposal to give the commissioner power to protect orphans.

In November, 1912, she went to New York to lecture on "Society's Responsibility for Crime." Miss Barnard lectured before the City Club of New York, League of Political Education of New York, Cooper Union Institute, exclusive girls' schools and colleges. In Boston, she spoke at Ford Hall and Faneuil Hall. She addressed a governors' congress at Richmond in 1913, and made the closing address before the American section of the International Tuberculosis Conference in Washington. She was voted a member of the American Academy of Social and Political Science in recognition of her contribution to constructive statecraft.

Kate Barnard was a slender, graceful, and pretty woman, with dark hair and skin and flashing eyes and a rapid-fire manner of speech that was the "despair of reporters." Her followers looked upon her as akin to Joan of Arc.

She said of Starr: "I have studied men until I know from the shape of their hands and head, the gait of their walk and the contour of their faces, much of their mode of life and the character of their thoughts . . . and Starr has made one of the sincerest efforts at reformation of all the 20,000 convicts I have known."

His parole was granted March 15, 1919, almost the moment the recommendations reached the office of Oklahoma's new governor, J. B. A. Robertson.

And the last week in June, Starr was again "called for" by officers of Bentonville, Arkansas, for the robbery of their bank twenty-six years before. Governor Robertson promptly rejected the requisition.[1]

Starr drifted back to Tulsa. Two items in the files of the First National Bank of Tulsa, today one of the state's largest such institutions, tell the saga of Oklahoma's famous badman in the months that followed.

A signature card shows that on July 25, four days short of the bank's 24th anniversary, Starr came in and deposited $80. Apparently he was playing it straight, making enough, somehow, to get by in 1919.

An envelope in the bank's files is from the office of W. P. "Waite" Phillips, Tulsa oil man and philanthropist, whose office was in the First National building. Some ten years later he became chairman of the bank. In the envelope is an IOU, dated October 1, 1919, from Starr to Phillips for $100.

The yellowed documents do not indicate whether Phillips ever collected on the IOU. It is assumed he did, for, by that time, Starr listed his occupation as "moving pictures."[2]

"There's more money in the motion picture business than in robbing banks," Tulsa friends remarked to Starr after paying twenty-five cents to see May B. Young in *Sweet Sixteen*. "Ex-waitresses and soda jerkers are getting rich in the movie game at Los Angeles. It should be a cinch for a famous bandit."[3]

The movie industry already was a factor that had given Tulsans the dream of a new Hollywood-on-the-Arkansas. In March, 1912, William Smith, who became a Tulsa theater magnate before his untimely death in October, 1925, had bought a $500 machine and begun making pictures in which local characters·and scenes were featured. A second venture was launched in 1913, with E. N. Adams, assistant secretary of the Commercial Club, as manager. In April, 1915, Tulsa landed an even more "stupendous project "—the Tulsa Motion Picture Company, under the leadership of H. A. Mackle. That summer, Frank Patterson, president of the Longhorn Film Company, made an appearance in Tulsa as a guest of Scout Younger, who had just made a three-reel film portraying the "true life" of the Younger brothers.

Just where Scout fitted into the Younger outlaw family has never been explained, but Scout was a friend of Emmett Dalton, last survivor of the Dalton gang at Coffeyville. The two of them had made at least one movie together titled *On the Texas Border,* and Emmett was a house guest of Scout's while in the city making personal appearances and narrating the film at the Empire theater.

Scout's movie, *The Younger Brothers,* came to Tulsa a few months later and was booked at the Lyric theater for two big days, February 28–29, 1916. Tulsans paid five and ten cents admission, and flocked to take another look at familiar landmarks and faces of the area.

As the industry became more permanent, a regular Western street of false fronts was established on the Sand Springs Road, and a succession of movies were produced at the studios there.

Smith was still the principal mover in the industry, but he soon faced serious competition in the person of Henry Starr. Starr acquired one-fourth interest in the Pan-American Motion Picture Company of Tulsa, which had been given a permit by the state to sell $120,000 worth of stock.[4]

Henry went into the business with vim and vigor. The company moved into Stroud to produce a silent film, *A Debtor to the Law,* depicting the double bank robbery, the most spectacular in Oklahoma history. Henry portrayed himself. Something of a hero, he lined up bank employees and townspeople to re-enact the scenes, even down to getting shot by Paul Curry.

The movie was an immediate success. Henry was the "Evening Starr" in a couple of pictures that followed. He was alleged to have netted, for his part, $15,000.

But he was unable to collect his profits. He received a flattering offer from a California concern to stage a bank robbery for one of their screenplays. The offer also indicated that possibly they would engage him as "technical director" for several other Westerns. Starr turned it down.

"He threw away a wonderful opportunity," George Davis, a well-known picture executive, said afterwards.

Starr could not go to California for fear Arkansas authorities would start new extradition proceedings, and during his tour with *A Debtor to the Law,* he had met Hulda Starr, a 23-year-old Sallisaw girl, no relation. They were married February 22, 1920, and went to Claremore.

In June, Henry called on Kate Barnard at the Cadillac Hotel in Oklahoma City.

"Kate," he said, "I want to borrow $100 to help me get back on my feet." He told her how he had been cheated, and the $100 would enable him to carry on his fight against the picture company.

Kate gave him $20. Then she went to a local attorney and asked him to help Henry collect the funds due him. The attorney promised he would do so, or see that Governor Robertson revoked the company's license.

It was the last time she heard from Starr. Supposedly,

the attorney's efforts failed, for Starr blamed pressing debts, including a bill of $1,200 production expense, for his ultimate downfall.

The last report from Starr on file in the state pardon and parole office was written November 1, 1920, in which he stated that he was trying to sell his one-fourth interest in the movies in which he took part.

The first week of February, 1921, he visited his son, a high-school senior, at Muskogee. He discussed his past with the boy at length, as he had on several occasions since his release from prison. This time he told his son: "Profit by my mistakes, Ted, and always live your life in a clean, straight manner. Crime cannot succeed. All young men should know crime is a losing game no matter who the players may be. Never start a life of crime. Once a fellow falls, it's hard to rise again. I've always expected to die with my boots on." [5]

Perhaps it was Indian superstitution that warned Starr of the fulfillment of his romantic prediction. Back at Claremore, he called his wife to him and put his arms around her.

"Honey," he said, "if I should die would you have me buried?"

"Of course, Henry," Hulda told him. "Why do you ask such a question?"

"Well"—he hesitated, with a peculiar look in his eyes—"I've always had a horror of just being dumped in the ground. I want to be put away proper."

Then he kissed her goodbye, straightened his shoulders resolutely, and left hurriedly, without looking back.[6]

Friday morning, February 18, Starr, with three companions in a high-powered touring car, drove into Harrison, Arkansas, a prosperous little Ozark community in

Boone county, sixty miles southeast of Bentonville. They circled the town first and cut all communications wires, then entered the People's National Bank.

Starr gathered up about $6,000, and ordered Cashier G. C. Hoffman to open the safe. When the bandits entered, brandishing revolvers, W. J. Meyers, aged 60, former president of the bank and a stockholder, was standing near the vault. Unseen by Starr, he "stepped into the darkness of the recess" and grasped a rifle secreted there for just such a purpose. The vault was used for keeping books and bank papers, the safe being used for currency. Cashier Hoffman stooped to open the safe as directed, Starr prodding him with his six-shooter and his companions keeping the other occupants of the bank covered. Starr, in his anxiety, stooped over to watch Hoffman closely, and at that moment Meyers fired.

The bullet struck Starr in the right side below the ribs and passed through his spine. He fell to the floor, paralyzed, and was overpowered before he could use his weapon. His companions fled from the building, jumped into their car, and sped south. They obtained no money. Starr had stuffed all the available cash into his pockets when he ordered the cashier to open the safe.[7]

A posse formed quickly and started in pursuit, "holding the bandits in sight for two miles when they stopped, set fire to their automobile and rushed into the woods." Sheriff J. Sibley Johnson immediately threw a cordon around the area, but the fugitives had vanished completely. The posse returned to Harrison late Friday night, "spent and hopeless of making a capture."[8]

At the jail, Starr refused to identify his companions. "I cannot talk of them," he said. Physicians extracted the bullet and expressed the opinion he would recover, but

Starr persisted in his conviction that he had only a short time to live. He sent his wife a telegram, telling her he was dying.

On Saturday, he rallied to an extent that he hoped for recovery. But early Sunday, he began to grow weaker and again abandoned hope. At 11 o'clock Tuesday morning, he lapsed into unconsciousness. A few hours later, he was dead. His wife Hulda, Starr's aged mother, and his 17-year-old son were at his side. They accompanied his body to Dewey, Oklahoma, for burial. A Boone county grand jury meeting to indict him on a bank robbery charge adjourned, and in Oklahoma his parole from the state penitentiary had been revoked by Governor Robertson.

Kate Barnard had become ill the latter part of 1920 and gone to Denver for hospital care. During her absence, she was not silent, and inveighed constantly about crime and social conditions. When she heard of Starr's death, she promptly, with characteristic vigor, lashed out with a damning indictment of society in general and the motion picture company in particular:

"The company which cheated Henry Starr out of the proceeds of his picture is directly responsible for the robbery in which he was shot and for his failure to travel the straight path. This company, however, is but an example of society at large, which seeks to destroy the man whose foot has slipped, instead of helping him to beat his way back to clean living. . . . It is but an example of the attitude of society toward former convicts.

"The fall of Starr will undo much of the good that has been done by those active in prison reform, because he was one of the outstanding figures in the criminal history of the nation and hundreds of criminals follow his example. But it will show the world, as probably nothing else can, the need of a state agency for reclaiming those who have taken the wrong road . . . the utter uselessness and costliness of trying to destroy a criminal instead of helping him.

"I have known Starr for many years. I know things about him that no one else on earth knows, and I know that whatever he has done, he has done it thinking from his misguided standpoint that he was doing right. He thought his criminal acts were right, for he was but striking back at society which had proven itself its enemy.

"As long as society maintains its present attitude toward criminals, just so long will society force men who want to play square back into a life of crime, as it forced Starr. . . ."

Kate Barnard apparently was utterly discouraged and taken aback. "It seems useless to try and help anyone in this greedy world," she concluded. "It is enough to make Heaven weep. . . . May God help us all." [9]

Most people agreed with her in the fact that, when they buried Henry Starr in the little cemetery at Dewey, Oklahoma, February 23, 1921, there ended the story of an outlaw as picturesque as any who ever poked a six-gun under the nose of a scared, small-town bank cashier in all the Western country. In the thirty years he had followed the bandit trade, he had more holdups to his credit than the James-Younger, Dalton-Doolin gangs combined.

Even Henry himself seemed a little proud of his record. The day before he died, he boasted to his doctors at Harrison, Arkansas:

"I've robbed more banks than any man in America."

Notes

CHAPTER I

[1] *Story of Crime Life of Henry Starr as Told by the Famous Bandit*. Published serially in the Wichita *Eagle*, February 27–March 4, 1921. (Hereafter noted as *Crime Life*).

[2] The Missouri, Kansas and Texas (Katy) railroad crossed the Indian Territory from Chetopa, Kansas, to Denison, Texas; the St. Louis-San Francisco (Frisco) had reached Vinita from Seneca, Missouri, in 1871, and was building southwest across the Cherokee Nation. Later, the Missouri-Pacific (Iron Mountain line) built south from Coffeyville, Kansas, through the Cherokee Nation via Wagoner and Fort Gibson to Van Buren and Fort Smith, Arkansas.

[3] Starr to the Fort Smith *Weekly Elevator*, October 18.

[4] *Thrilling Events, Life of Henry Starr*. Famous Cherokee Indian outlaw narrates his many adventures from boyhood to date. Written in the Colorado Penitentiary by Himself. Published July, 1914. (N.p.) Pp. 1–5, 9–10.

[5] Lewis R. Walker (no relation to C. N.), a 74-year-old barber of Miami, Oklahoma, who, as a boy, attended the Cherokee Male Seminary at Tahlequah, recalled in 1956: "One of my schoolmates was Henry Starr. He was one of the large boys of the school, always wanting to fight, seemed to crave excitement. In fact, he was expelled from school for fighting. Another boy at the school was going to give Henry a haircut. He ran the clippers right down the middle of Henry's head. That is what started it." As a young man, Walker served with the mounted Indian police.

CHAPTER II

[1] *Thrilling Events*, p. 5.

[2] *Ibid.*

[3] The records show that Starr was not placed in jail until February 13, 1892.

[4] *Thrilling Events,* pp. 6–8.

[5] *Op. cit.,* February 28.

[6] Pp. 10–11.

[7] *Op. cit.,* March 2.

[8] Starr was indicted by a federal grand jury in September and his trail set for November 23, 1892.

[9] *Thrilling Events,* pp. 11–12.

[10] During this phase of his career, Starr has been credited with riding with the Cook gang and Cherokee Bill, "taking part with them in several minor holdups and store robberies." (Paul I. Wellman, *A Dynasty of Western Outlaws,* p. 254; Harry Sinclair Drago, *Outlaws on Horseback,* pps. 165, 175–76). The facts do not support such statements. Starr's only association with this so-called criminal "dynasty" was nearly a year later, in the Fort Smith federal jail.

CHAPTER III

[1] *Starr v. United States,* Case #1080, May 14, 1894; S. W. Harman, *Hell on the Border; He Hanged Eighty-eight Men,* p. 370.

[2] *Crime Life, op cit.,* March 3.

[3] Coffeyville *Daily Journal,* December 14, 1892; Vinita *Indian Chieftain,* December 15, 1892.

[4] P. 12.

[5] Vinita *Indian Chieftain,* December 15, 1892.

[6] Numerous versions of the slaying of Wilson by Starr have been written, ranging from pure fiction to the ridiculous. Mostly they have been based on accounts in Fred Sutton's *Hands Up!,* pp. 243–44, and E. D. Nix's *Oklahombres,* pp. 117–18. Harry Sinclair Drago obviously relies on the Sutton account in *Outlaws on Horseback,* pp. 291–92. The facts can be found in *Starr v. United States, op. cit.*

[7] Pp. 12–13.

[8] *Op. cit.,* March 3.

CHAPTER IV

[1] *Crime Life, op. cit.,* March 4.

[2] *Thrilling Events,* p. 13.

[3] *Crime Life, op. cit.,* February 27.

[4] *Thrilling Events,* p. 14.

[5] *Crime Life, op. cit.,* February 27.

⁶ *Ibid.*, March 4.

⁷ Stillwater *Gazette*, November 11, 1892; Fort Smith *Weekly Elevator*, January 27, 1893; Glenn Shirley, *Heck Thomas, Frontier Marshal*, pp. 155–57.

⁸ Vinita *Indian Chieftain*, April 20, 1893; Shirley, *op. cit.*, pp. 158–59.

⁹ *Crime Life, op. cit.*, March 4.

¹⁰ *Ibid.*

¹¹ *Thrilling Events*, pp. 13–14; *Crime Life, op. cit.*, March 4; Osage *Journal*, February 24, 1921; W. B. Lawson, *Hank Starr, The Log Cabin Bandit*, pp. 2–3; Recollections of W. A. Hancock, Indian-Pioneer History, Vol. 4, pp. 273–74, Oklahoma State Historical Society.

¹² *Thrilling Events*, p. 13.

¹³ Recollections of Ben F. Williams, Indian-Pioneer History, Vol. 49, pp. 435–36, Oklahoma State Historical Society.

¹⁴ *Thrilling Events*, pp. 14–16.

¹⁵ Sutton, *op. cit.*, p. 246.

¹⁶ Pp. 16–17.

¹⁷ *Ibid.*

CHAPTER V

¹ *Thrilling Events*, pp. 17–18.

² *Ibid.*, p. 19.

³ *Ibid.*, p. 20.

⁴ Harman, *op. cit.*, p. 371.

⁵ *Thrilling Events*, p. 21.

⁶ *Ibid.*

⁷ Fort Smith *Weekly Elevator*, May 5, 1893.

⁸ *Thrilling Events*, pp. 21–22.

⁹ *Ibid.*, p. 23.

¹⁰ *Ibid.*, pp. 23–24; Bentonville *Sun*, June 7, 1893; Harman, *op. cit.*, pp. 364–65; Recollections of R. Y. Nance, County Judge of Benton County, Indian-Pioneer History, Vol. 7, pp. 398–99, Oklahoma State Historical Society; Recollections of Jim Craig, "The Day They Robbed the Bank of Bentonville," Tulsa *World*, August 14, 1960.

CHAPTER VI

¹ *Thrilling Events*, p. 24.

² Recollections of, *op. cit.*

³ *Thrilling Events*, p. 24.
⁴ Recollections of, *op. cit.*
⁵ *Thrilling Events*, p. 25.
⁶ South McAlester *Capital,* July 19, 1894; Ardmore *State Herald,* July 19, 1894; Eufaula *Indian Journal,* July 20, 1894.
⁷ *Daily Oklahoma State Capital,* June 13, 1893; *ibid.,* June 17, 1893.
⁸ *Thrilling Events*, p. 25.
⁹ *Ibid.,* p. 26. The statement of Drago, *op cit.,* p. 294, that "Starr married a girl named Mary Jones, a Cherokee mix-blood [*sic*]" is incorrect.
¹⁰ See also Vinita *Indian Chieftain,* July 6, 1893; Tahlequah *Cherokee Advocate,* July 8, 1893; Harman, *op. cit.,* pp. 365–66.
¹¹ P. 26.
¹² *Thrilling Events*, p. 28.
¹³ *Ibid.*

CHAPTER VII

¹ *Thrilling Events*, p. 23.
² Vinita *Indian Chieftain,* July 27, 1893.
³ *Ibid.,* October 26, 1893; Fort Smith *Daily Record,* August 12, 1893.
⁴ Vinita *Indian Chieftain,* November 3, 1893.
⁵ *Ibid.,* July 27, 1893.
⁶ *Ibid.,* October 5, 1893; Guthrie *Daily Leader,* October 22, 1893.
⁷ *Weekly Oklahoma State Capital,* November 4, 1893.
⁸ Pp. 29–30.
⁹ *Ibid.*
¹⁰ *United States v. Henry Starr,* Case No. 74, Circuit Court, Western District of Arkansas.
¹¹ *Thrilling Events*, p. 30.
¹² Vinita *Indian Chieftain,* October 26, 1893.
¹³ *Ibid.; Starr v. United States, op. cit.*
¹⁴ *Starr v. United States, op. cit.*
¹⁵ Self. Tr. 160.
¹⁶ *Starr v. United States, op. cit.*
¹⁷ *Ibid.*
¹⁸ *Op. cit.,* pp. 166–67.
¹⁹ P. 126.
²⁰ P. 31.
²¹ Fort Smith *Weekly Elevator,* November 10, 1893.

²² *Starr v. United States,* Case #1080, May 14, 1894.

CHAPTER VIII

¹ *Thrilling Events,* p. 31.
² Harman, *op. cit.,* p. 402.
³ Fort Smith *Weekly Elevator,* February 1, 1895.
⁴ Vinita *Indian Chieftain,* July 18, 1895.
⁵ *Op. cit.,* pp. 162–63.
⁶ *Op. cit.,* pp. 3–4.
⁷ *Op. cit.,* p. 186.
⁸ P. 31.
⁹ The details of Keating's murder and the surrender of Cherokee Bill appear in the Vinita *Indian Chieftain,* Fort Smith *Democrat,* South McAlester *Capital,* and Atoka *Indian Citizen,* August 1, 1895, and Harman, *op. cit.,* pp. 403–06. Drago is mistaken in stating the two weapons smuggled in to Cherokee Bill were ".41-caliber pistols." The revolver found in the bucket of lime was a forty-five, and Keating was killed with a thirty-eight.
¹⁰ Fort Smith *Democrat,* August 29, 1895; South McAlester *Capital,* September 5, 1895; Ardmore *State Herald,* September 12, 1895; Harman, *op. cit.,* p. 407, pp. 436–39.
¹¹ South McAlester *Capital,* September 5, 1895; Ardmore *State Herald,* September 12, 1895.
¹² *Thrilling Events,* p. 32.
¹³ Vinita *Indian Chieftain,* September 19, 1895.
¹⁴ *Starr v. United States,* Case #389, January 4, 1897, 164 U. S. 627.
¹⁵ *Ibid.*
¹⁶ *Quinn v. State,* 55 Oklahoma Criminal Reports 116; *Pittman v. State,* 8 Oklahoma Criminal Reports 58; *Wettengel v. State,* 30 Oklahoma Criminal Reports 388.
¹⁷ Pp. 32–34.
¹⁸ *United States v. Henry Starr,* Case. No. 74, *op. cit.,* Indictment #3724.
¹⁹ *Ibid.,* Indictment #3725 (Counts 1, 3, 4, 5, 7, 9, and 10, on which Starr received 1 year and 1 day each).
²⁰ *Ibid.,* Indictment #2724.
²¹ *Thrilling Events,* p. 35.
²² Tahlequah *Cherokee Advocate,* December 7, 1901.
²³ Joint Resolution No. 5, p. 154, Record of Laws, 1901 (Cherokee–Pardons, Indian Archives Division, Oklahoma Historical Society).

[24] Vinita *Indian Chieftain,* April 10, 1902.

[25] *Daily Oklahoman,* January 21, 1903; Tahlequah *Cherokee Advocate,* January 24, 1903.

CHAPTER IX

[1] Vinita *Daily Chieftain,* September 16, 1903; Tahlequah *Cherokee Advocate* September 19, 1903.

[2] Tulsa *World,* March 29, 1915.

[3] *Thrilling Events,* p. 46.

[4] *Ibid.,* pp. 47–48.

[5] Guthrie *Daily Leader,* March 19, 1908; Shawnee *Daily Herald,* March 20, 1908; Eufaula *Indian Journal,* March 27, 1908.

[6] *Thrilling Events,* pp. 35–38.

[7] *Ibid.,* p. 38. This is contrary to Drago, *op. cit.,* p. 296, who claims Starr "collected several thousand dollars," was captured by a sheriff's posse "east of Lamar" and sent to the Canon City penitentiary for twenty-five years.

[8] Lawson, *op. cit.,* p. 4.

[9] *Thrilling Events,* p. 44.

[10] *Ibid.,* p. 49.

[11] *Ibid.,* pp. 49–51.

[12] Warden Harry C. Tinsley to G. S., August 19, 1954, Records of the Colorado State Penitentiary, *re* Henry Starr, No. 7613.

CHAPTER X

[1] Eufaula *Indian Journal,* March 5, 1915.

[2] *Daily Oklahoman,* March 2, 1915.

[3] Eufaula *Indian Journal,* April 2, 1915.

[4] Drago, *op. cit.,* p. 297, claims only six, states that "they turned into the hitch-rack in front of a store less than half a block from the two banks," and incorrectly identifies two as the later notorious Al Spencer and his brother-in-law, Grover Durrell.

[5] *Op. cit.,* pp. 262–63.

[6] *Op. cit.,* p. 299.

[7] *Daily Oklahoman,* March 29, 1915.

[8] *Ibid.,* March 30, 1915; Chandler *News-Publicist,* April 2, 1915.

[9] Chandler *News-Publicist,* April 16, 1915.

[10] *Ibid.*

[11] *Ibid.,* July 23, 1915.

[12] *Ibid.,* August 6, 1915.

[13] *Ibid.,* August 13, 1915.

[14] Warden Jerome J. Waters, Jr. to G. S., August 17, 1954, Records of the Oklahoma State Penitentiary.

CHAPTER XI

[1] *Daily Oklahoman,* July 3, 1919.
[2] *Tulsa World,* July 29, 1962.
[3] Lawson, *op. cit.,* p. 6.
[4] Russell Gideon, "Hollywood-on-the-Arkansas," *Tulsa World,* April 1, 1962.
[5] *Osage Journal,* February 24, 1921.
[6] *Daily Oklahoman,* February 23, 1921.
[7] *Ibid.,* February 19, 1921.
[8] *Ibid.,* February 21, 1921.
[9] *Ibid.,* February 23, 1921.

Index

201

Blackstone Switch, 122
Blue Duck, 7
Blue River, 3
Booker, D. E., 65
Boone, Nathan, 3
Boone County, Ark., 189-190
Bosque, Ariz., 159
Boston, Mass., 184
Braggs, Cherokee Nation, 124
Breeding, H. E., 168, 170
Bristow, Okla., 173-174
Brizzolara, James, 136
Brooklyn, N. Y., 77, 149
Bruce, I. W., 80
Bruner, Heck, 76, 130
Buck gang, 7
Buffington, T. W., 144
Butterfield overland stage, 6
Byars State Bank, 163

Caddo, Choctaw Nation, 65
Caddo Reservation, 157
Cain, Bill, 65
California Creek, 31, 38
Caney, Kans., 46-47, 51-52, 150
Caney *Daily Chronicle,* 47, 51-52
Caney Valley Bank, 47
Cannon, Rufus, 37-38
Canon City, Colo., 160
Canton, F. M., 173
Carney, Okla., 165, 178, 180
Carney State Bank, 163-164, 178
Catlin, George, 3
Catoosa, Cherokee Nation, 124
Chandler, Okla., 124, 168, 172-175, 177, 179
Chandler *News-Publicist,* 164, 172
Charles, J. B., Jr., 168
Chastain, W. A., 169
Chaves County, New Mex., 124
Cheney, Alf, 76-77
Cheney, Frank, 28, 40-41, 45-46, 54, 57, 59-60, 62-66

Cherokee Indians, 2-3, 20
Cherokee Nation, 3-5, 35, 38, 64, 66, 148, 150, 166
Cherokee National Council, 141, 143
Cherokee Outlet, 38
Chickasaw Nation, 38
Choctaw Nation, 65
Christie, Ned, 7
Cimarron River, 166
Citizens' State Bank of Wardville, 163
City Club of New York, 184
Claremore, Okla., 187-188
Clarksville, Tex., 65
Clay County, Tex., 124
Clayton, W. H. H., 72, 136
Cleveland, Grover, 66, 80
Coffeyville, Kans., 14, 31-32, 66, 186
Coffin, E. G., 141
Collier, Carroll, 30
Collin County, Tex., 65
Collins, Frank, 74
Colorado Springs, Colo., 67, 74
Columbus, Ohio, 140-143
Commercial Club (of Tulsa), 186
Commonwealth v. Selfridge, 105
Cook, James, 123
Cook, William Tuttle ("Bill Cook, The Famous Outlaw"), 123-124, 126-127
Cook gang, 7, 122-124
Cooper Union Institute, 184
Craig, Jim, 63-64
Craig, R. E., 41
Craig & Son's store, 59, 61
Cravens, William M., 72, 141
Creek Nation, 124, 156
Creekmore, Milo, 26-28, 38-39, 74, 77-78
Crime Life, 22, 26, 33
Croxdale, Clint, 61

206